The Cambridge Manuals of Science and
Literature

T0352317

THE BEAUTIFUL

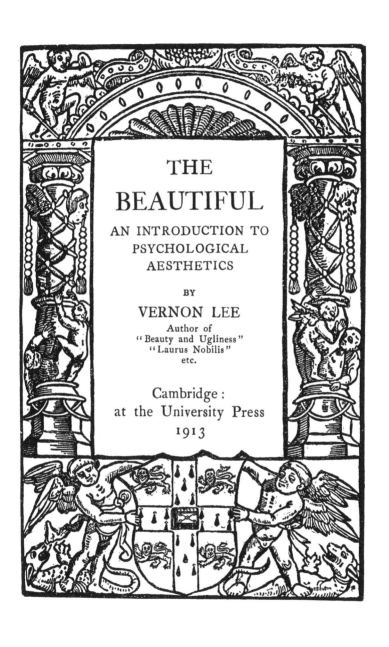

THE

BEAUTIFUL

AN INTRODUCTION TO PSYCHOLOGICAL AESTHETICS

BY

VERNON LEE

Author of
"Beauty and Ugliness"
"Laurus Nobilis"
etc.

Cambridge :
at the University Press
1913

CAMBRIDGE UNIVERSITY PRESS
Cambridge, New York, Melbourne, Madrid, Cape Town,
Singapore, São Paulo, Delhi, Tokyo, Mexico City

Cambridge University Press
The Edinburgh Building, Cambridge CB2 8RU, UK

Published in the United States of America by
Cambridge University Press, New York

www.cambridge.org
Information on this title: www.cambridge.org/9781107401662

© Cambridge University Press 1913

First published 1913
First paperback edition 2011

A catalogue record for this publication is available from the British Library

ISBN 978-1-107-40166-2 Paperback

*With the exception of the coat of arms
at the foot, the design on the title page is a
reproduction of one used by the earliest known
Cambridge printer, John Siberch, 1521*

PREFACE AND APOLOGY

I HAVE tried in this little volume to explain æsthetic preference, particularly as regards visible shapes, by the facts of mental science. But my explanation is addressed to readers in whom I have no right to expect a previous knowledge of psychology, particularly in its more modern developments. I have therefore based my explanation of the problems of æsthetics as much as possible upon mental facts familiar, or at all events easily intelligible, to the lay reader. Now mental facts thus available are by no means the elementary processes with which analytical and, especially experimental, psychology has dealings. They are, on the contrary, the everyday, superficial and often extremely confused views which practical life and its wholly unscientific vocabulary present of those ascertained or hypothetical scientific facts. I have indeed endeavoured (for instance in the analysis of perception as distinguished from sensation) to impart some rudiments of psychology in the course of my æsthetical explanation, and I have avoided, as much as possible, misleading the reader about such fearful complexes and cruxes as *memory*, *association* and *imagination*.

But I have been obliged to speak in terms intelligible to the lay reader, and I am fully aware that these terms correspond only very approximately to what is, or at present passes as, psychological fact. I would therefore beg the psychologist (to whom I offer this little volume as a possible slight addition even to his stock of facts and hypotheses) to understand that in speaking, for instance, of Empathy as involving a *thought* of certain activities, I mean merely that whatever happens has the same result *as if we thought*; and that the processes, whatever they may be (also in the case of measuring, comparing and co-ordinating), translate themselves, *when they are detected*, into *thoughts*; but that I do not in the least pre-judge the question whether the processes, the "thoughts," the measuring, comparing etc. exist on subordinate planes of consciousness or whether they are mainly physiological and only occasionally abutting in conscious resultants. Similarly, lack of space and the need for clearness have obliged me to write as if shape-preference invariably necessitated the detailed process of ocular perception, instead of being due, as is doubtless most often the case, to every kind of associative abbreviation and equivalence of processes.

VERNON LEE

Maiano *near* Florence,
  Easter 1913.

CONTENTS

THE BEAUTIFUL

CHAPTER I

THE ADJECTIVE "BEAUTIFUL"

THIS little book, like the great branch of mental science to which it is an introduction, makes no attempt to "form the taste" of the public and still less to direct the doings of the artist. It deals not with *ought* but with *is*, leaving to Criticism the inference from the latter to the former. It does not pretend to tell how things can be made beautiful or even how we can recognise that things *are* beautiful. It takes Beauty as already existing and enjoyed, and seeks to analyse and account for Beauty's existence and enjoyment. More strictly speaking, it analyses and accounts for Beauty not inasmuch as existing in certain objects and processes, but rather as calling forth (and being called forth by) a particular group of mental activities and habits. It does not ask : What are the peculiarities of the things (and the proceedings) which we call *Beautiful ?* but : What are the peculiarities of our thinking and feeling when in the presence of a thing to which we apply this adjective ?   The study of single beautiful things, and even more, the comparison of various categories thereof, is indeed one-half of all scientific æsthetics, but only inasmuch as it adds to our knowledge of the particular mental activities which such " Beautiful " (and vice versâ " Ugly ") things elicit in us.   For it is on the nature of this active response on our own part that depends the application of those terms *Beautiful* and *Ugly* in every single instance ;   and indeed their application in any instances whatsoever, their very existence in the human vocabulary.

In accordance with this programme I shall not start with a formal definition of the word *Beautiful*, but ask : on what sort of occasions we make use of it.   Evidently, on *occasions when we feel satisfaction rather than dissatisfaction*, satisfaction meaning willingness either to prolong or to repeat the particular experience which has called forth that word ;   and meaning also that if it comes to a choice between two or several experiences, we *prefer* the experience thus marked by the word *Beautiful*. *Beautiful*, we may therefore formulate, *implies on our part an attitude of satisfaction and preference*. But there are other words which imply that much ; first and foremost the words, in reality synonyms, USEFUL and GOOD.   I call these synonyms because *good* always implies *good for*, or *good in*, that is to say fitness for a purpose, even though that purpose may be masked under *conforming to a standard* or *obeying a commandment*, since the standard or commandment represents not the caprice of a community, a race or a divinity, but some (real or imaginary) utility of a less immediate kind. So much for the meaning of *good* when implying standards and commandments ; ninety-nine times out of a hundred there is, however, no such implication, and *good* means nothing more than *satisfactory in the way of use and advantage*. Thus a *good* road is a road we prefer because it takes us to our destination quickly and easily. A *good* speech is one we prefer because it succeeds in explaining or persuading. And a *good* character (good friend, father, husband, citizen) is one that gives satisfaction by the fulfilment of moral obligations.

But note the difference when we come to *Beautiful*. A *beautiful* road is one we prefer because it affords views we like to look at ; its being devious and inconvenient will not prevent its being *beautiful*. A *beautiful* speech is one we like to hear or remember, although it may convince or persuade neither us nor anybody. A *beautiful* character is one we like to think about but which may never practically help anyone, if for instance, it exists not in real life but in a novel. Thus the adjective *Beautiful* implies *an attitude of preference, but not an attitude of present or future turning to our purposes*. There is even a significant lack of symmetry in the words employed (at all events in English, French and German) to distinguish what we like from what we dislike in the way of weather. For weather which makes us uncomfortable and hampers our comings and goings by rain, wind or mud, is described as *bad*; while the opposite kind of weather is called *beautiful*, *fine*, or *fair*, as if the greater comfort, convenience, usefulness of such days were forgotten in the lively satisfaction afforded to our mere contemplation.

Our mere contemplation! Here we have struck upon the main difference between our attitude when we use the word *good* or *useful*, and when we use the word *beautiful*. And we can add to our partial formula " beautiful implies satisfaction and preference "—the distinguishing predicate—" *of a contemplative kind.*" This general statement will be confirmed by an everyday anomaly in our use of the word beautiful; and the examination of this seeming exception will not only exemplify what I have said about our attitude when employing that word, but add to this information the name of the emotion corresponding with that attitude: the emotion of *admiration*. For the selfsame object or proceeding may sometimes be called *good* and sometimes *beautiful*, according as the mental attitude is practical or contemplative. While we admonish the traveller to take a certain road because he will find it *good*, we may hear that same road described by an enthusiastic coachman as *beautiful*, *anglicè fine* or *splendid*, because there is no question of immediate use, and the road's qualities are merely being contemplated with admiration. Similarly, we have all of us heard an engineer apply to a piece of machinery, and even a surgeon to an operation, the apparently far-fetched adjective Beautiful, or one of the various equivalents, fine, splendid, glorious (even occasionally *jolly !*) by which Englishmen express their admiration. The change of word represents a change of attitude. The engineer is no longer bent upon using the machine, nor the surgeon estimating the advantages of the operation. Each of these highly practical persons has switched off his practicality, if but for an imperceptible fraction of time and in the very middle of a practical estimation or even of practice itself. The machine or operation, the skill, the inventiveness, the fitness for its purposes, are being considered *apart from action*, and advantage, means and time, to-day or yesterday ; *platonically* we may call it from the first great teacher of æsthetics. They are being, in one word, contemplated with admiration. And *admiration* is the rough and ready name for the mood, however transient, for the emotion, however faint, wherewith we greet whatever makes us contemplate, because contemplation happens to give satisfaction. The satisfaction may be a mere skeleton of the " I'd rather than not " description ; or it may be a massive alteration in our being, radiating far beyond the present, evoking from the past similar conditions to corroborate it ; storing itself up for the future ; penetrating, like the joy of a fine day, into our animal spirits, altering pulse, breath, gait, glance and demeanour ; and transfiguring our whole momentary outlook on life. But, superficial or overwhelming, *this kind of satisfaction connected with the word Beautiful is always of the Contemplative order*.

And upon the fact we have thus formulated depend, as we shall see, most of the other facts and formulæ of our subject.

This essentially unpractical attitude accompanying the use of the word *Beautiful* has led metaphysical æstheticians to two famous, and I think, quite misleading theories. The first of these defines æsthetic appreciation as *disinterested interest*, gratuitously identifying self-interest with the practical pursuit of advantages we have not yet got ; and overlooking the fact that such appreciation implies enjoyment and is so far the very reverse of disinterested. The second philosophical theory (originally Schiller's, and revived by Herbert Spencer) takes advantage of the non-practical attitude connected with the word *Beautiful* to define art and its enjoyment as a kind of *play*. Now although leisure and freedom from cares are necessary both for play and for æsthetic appreciation, the latter differs essentially from the former by its contemplative nature. For although it may be possible to watch *other people* playing football or chess or bridge in a purely con-templative spirit and with the deepest admiration, even as the engineer or surgeon may contemplate the perfections of a machine or an operation, yet the concentration on the aim and the next moves constitutes on the part of the players *themselves* an eminently practical state of mind, one diametri-cally opposed to contemplation, as I hope to make evident in the next section.

CHAPTER II

CONTEMPLATIVE SATISFACTION

WE have thus defined the word *Beautiful* as implying an attitude of contemplative satisfaction, marked by a feeling, sometimes amounting to an *emotion*, of admiration; and so far contrasted it with the practical attitude implied by the word *good*. But we require to know more about the distinctive peculiarities of contemplation as such, by which, moreover, it is distinguished not merely from the practical attitude, but also from the scientific one.

Let us get some rough and ready notions on this subject by watching the behaviour and listening to the remarks of three imaginary wayfarers in front of a view, which they severally consider in the practical, the scientific and the æsthetic manner. The view was from a hill-top in the neighbourhood of Rome or of Edinburgh, whichever the Reader can best realise; and in its presence the three travellers halted and remained for a moment absorbed each in his thoughts.

" It will take us a couple of hours to get home on foot "—began one of the three. " We might have been back for tea-time if only there had been a tram and a funicular. And that makes me think : Why not start a joint-stock company to build them ? There must be water-power in these hills ; the hill people could keep cows and send milk and butter to town. Also houses could be built for people whose work takes them to town, but who want good air for their children ; the hire-purchase system, you know. It might prove a godsend and a capital investment, though I suppose some people would say it spoilt the view. The idea is quite a *good* one. I shall get an expert—— "

" These hills," put in the second man—" are said to be part of an ancient volcano. I don't know whether that theory is *true* ! It would be *interesting* to examine whether the summits have been ground down in places by ice, and whether there are traces of volcanic action at different geological epochs ; the plain, I suppose, has been under the sea at no very distant period. It is also *interesting* to notice, as we can up here, how the situation of the town is explained by the river affording easier shipping on a coast poor in natural harbours ; moreover, this has been the inevitable meeting-place of sea-faring and pastoral populations. These investigations would prove, as I said, remarkably full of interest."

" I wish "—complained the third wayfarer, but probably only to himself—" I wish these men would hold their tongues and let one enjoy this exquisite place without diverting one's attention to *what might be done* or to *how it all came about.* They don't seem to feel how *beautiful* it all is." And he concentrated himself on contemplation of the landscape, his delight brought home by a stab of reluctance to leave.

Meanwhile one of his companions fell to wondering whether there really was sufficient pasture for dairy-farming and water-power for both tramway and funicular, and where the necessary capital could be borrowed ; and the other one hunted about for marks of stratification and upheaval, and ransacked his memory for historical data about the various tribes originally inhabiting that country.

" I suppose you're a painter and regretting you haven't brought your sketching materials ? " said the scientific man, always interested in the causes of phenomena, even such trifling ones as a man remaining quiet before a landscape.

" I reckon you are one of those literary fellows, and are planning out where you can use up a description of this place "—corrected the rapid insight of the practical man, accustomed to weigh people's motives in case they may be turned to use.

" I am *not* a painter, and I'm *not* a writer " —exclaimed the third traveller, " and I thank Heaven I'm not ! For if I were I might be trying to engineer a picture or to match adjectives, instead of merely enjoying all this beauty. Not but that I should like to have a sketch or a few words of description for when I've turned my back upon it. And Heaven help me, I really believe that when we are all back in London I may be quite glad to hear you two talking about your tramway-funicular company and your volcanic and glacial action, because your talk will evoke in my mind the remembrance of this place and moment which you have done your best to spoil for me ———"

" That's what it is to be æsthetic "—said the two almost in the same breath.

" And that, I suppose "—answered the third with some animosity—" is what you mean by being practical or scientific."

Now the attitude of mind of the practical man and of the man of science, though differing so obviously from one another (the first bent upon producing new and advantageous *results*, the second examining, without thought of advantage, into possible *causes*), both differed in the same way from the attitude of the man who was merely contemplating what he called the beauty of the scene. They were, as he complained, thinking of *what might be done* and of *how it had all come about*. That is to say they were both thinking *away* from that landscape. The scientific man actually turned his back to it in examining first one rock, then another. The practical man must have looked both at the plain in front and at the hill he was on, since he judged that there was pasture and water-power, and that the steepness required supplementing the tramway by a funicular. But besides the different items of landscape, and the same items under different angles, which were thus offered to these two men's bodily eyes, there was a far greater variety, and rapider succession of items and perspectives presented to the eyes of their spirit : the practical man's mental eye seeing not only the hills, plain, and town with details not co-existing in perspective or even in time, but tram-lines and funiculars in various stages of progress, dairy-products, pasture, houses, dynamos, waterfalls, offices, advertisements, cheques, etc., etc., and the scientific man's inner vision glancing with equal speed from volcanoes to ice-caps and seas in various stages of geological existence, besides minerals under the microscope, inhabitants in prehistoric or classic garb, let alone probably pages of books and interiors of libraries. Moreover, most, if not all these mental images (blocking out from attention the really existing landscape) could be called images only by courtesy, swished over by the mental eye as by an express train, only just enough seen to know what it was, or perhaps nothing seen at all, mere words filling up gaps in the chain of thought. So that what satisfaction there might be in the case was not due to these rapidly scampered through items, but to the very fact of getting to the next one, and to a looming, dominating goal, an ultimate desired result, to wit, pounds, shillings, and pence in the one case, and a coherent explanation in the other. In both cases equally there was a kaleidoscopic and cinematographic succession of aspects, but of aspects of which only one detail perhaps was noticed. Or, more strictly speaking, there was no interest whatever in aspects as such, but only in the possibilities of action which these aspects implied; whether actions future and personally profitable, like building tram-lines and floating joint-stock companies, or actions mainly past and quite impersonally interesting, like those of extinct volcanoes or prehistoric civilisations.

Now let us examine the mental attitude of the third man, whom the two others had first mistaken for an artist or writer, and then dismissed as an æsthetic person.

CHAPTER III

HAVING settled upon a particular point of view as
the one he liked best, he remained there in contemplation of the aspect it afforded him. Had he descended
another twenty minutes, or looked through power-
ful glasses, he would have seen the plain below as
a juxtaposition of emerald green, raw Sienna, and
pale yellow, whereas, at the distance where he chose
to remain, its colours fused into indescribably
lovely lilacs and russets. Had he moved freely
about he would have become aware that a fanlike
arrangement of sharply convergent lines, tempting
his eye to run rapidly into their various angles,
must be thought of as a chessboard of dikes, hedges,
and roads, dull as if drawn with a ruler on a slate.
Also that the foothills, instead of forming a monu-
mental mass with the mountains behind them, lay
in a totally different plane and distracted the
attention by their aggressive projection. While,
as if to spoil the aspect still more, he would have
been forced to recognise (as Ruskin explains by
his drawing of the cottage roof and the Matterhorn
peak) that the exquisitely phrased skyline of the

14

furthermost hills, picked up at rhythmical intervals
into sharp crests, dropping down merely to rush
up again in long concave curves, was merely an illusion of perspective, nearer lines seeming higher and
further ones lower, let alone that from a balloon
you would see only flattened mounds. But to how
things might look from a balloon, or under a microscope, that man did not give one thought, any more
than to how they might look after a hundred years
of tramways and funiculars or how they had looked
before thousands of years of volcanic and glacial
action. He was satisfied with the wonderfully
harmonised scheme of light and colour, the pattern
(more and more detailed, more and more co-ordinated
with every additional exploring glance) of keenly
thrusting, delicately yielding lines, meeting as
purposefully as if they had all been alive and executing some great, intricate dance. He did not concern
himself whether what he was looking at was an
aggregate of things ; still less what might be these
things' other properties. He was not concerned
with things at all, but only with a particular appearance (he did not care whether it answered to reality),
only with one (he did not want to know whether
there might be any other) *aspect*.

For, odd as it may sound, a *Thing* is both much
more and much less than an *Aspect*. Much more,
because a *Thing* really means not only qualities of

its own and reactions of ours which are actual and present, but a far greater number and variety thereof which are potential. Much *less*, on the other hand, because of these potential qualities and reactions constituting a Thing only a minimum need be thought of at any given time ; instead of which, an aspect is all there, its qualities closely interpendent, and our reactions entirely taken up in connecting them as whole and parts. A rose, for instance, is not merely a certain assemblage of curves and straight lines and colours, seen as the painter sees it, at a certain angle, petals masking part of stem, leaf protruding above bud : it is the possibility of other combinations of shapes, including those seen when the rose (or the person looking) is placed head downwards. Similarly it is the possibility of certain sensations of resistance, softness, moisture, pricking if we attempt to grasp it, of a certain fragrance if we breathe in the air. It is the possibility of turning into a particular fruit, with the possibility of our finding that fruit bitter and non-edible ; of being developed from cuttings, pressed in a book, made a present of or cultivated for lucre. Only one of these groups of possibilities may occupy our thoughts, the rest not glanced at, or only glanced at subsequently ; but if, on trial, any of these grouped possibilities disappoint us, we decide that this is not a real rose, but a paper rose, or a painted one, or no rose at all, but some *other thing*. For, so far as our consciousness is concerned, *things* are merely groups of actual and potential reactions on our own part, that is to say of expectations which experience has linked together in more or less stable groups. The practical man and the man of science in my fable, were both of them dealing with *Things* : passing from one group of potential reaction to another, hurrying here, dallying there, till of the actual *aspect* of the landscape there remained nothing in their thoughts, trams and funiculars in the future, volcanoes and icecaps in the past, having entirely altered all that ; only the material constituents and the geographical locality remaining as the unshifted item in those much pulled about bundles of thoughts of possibilities.

Every *thing* may have a great number of very different *Aspects* ; and some of these *Aspects* may invite contemplation, as that landscape invited the third man to contemplate it ; while other *aspects* (say the same place AFTER a proper course of tramways and funiculars and semi-detached residences, or *before* the needful volcanic and glacial action) may be such as are dismissed or slurred as fast as possible. Indeed, with the exception of a very few cubes not in themselves especially attractive, I cannot remember any *things* which do not present

B

quite as many displeasing aspects as pleasing ones. The most beautiful building is not beautiful if stood on its head; the most beautiful picture is not beautiful looked at through a microscope or from too far off; the most beautiful melody is not beautiful if begun at the wrong end. . . . Here the Reader may interrupt: " What nonsense ! Of course the building *is* a building only when right side up ; the picture isn't a picture any longer under a microscope ; the melody isn't a melody except begun at the beginning "—all which means that when we speak of a building, a picture, or a melody, we are already implicitly speaking, no longer of a *Thing*, but of one of the possible *Aspects* of a thing ; *and that when we say that a thing is beautiful, we mean that it affords one or more aspects which we contemplate with satisfaction.* But if a beautiful mountain or a beautiful woman could only be *contemplated*, if the mountain could not also be climbed or tunnelled, if the woman could not also get married, bear children and have (or not have !) a vote, we should say that the mountain and the woman were not *real things.* Hence we come to the conclusion, paradoxical only as long as we fail to define what we are talking about, *that what we contemplate as beautiful is an Aspect of a Thing, but never a Thing itself.* In other words : Beautiful is an adjective applicable to Aspects not to Things, or to Things only, inasmuch as we consider them as possessing (among other potentialities) beautiful Aspects. So that we can now formulate : *The word beautiful implies the satisfaction derived from the contemplation not of things but of aspects.*

This summing up has brought us to the very core of our subject ; and I should wish the Reader to get it by heart, until he grow familiarised therewith in the course of our further examinations. Before proceeding upon these, I would, however, ask him to reflect how this last formula of ours bears upon the old, seemingly endless, squabble as to whether or not beauty has anything to do with truth, and whether art, as certain moralists contend, is a school of lying. For *true* or *false* is a judgment of existence ; it refers to *Things* ; it implies that besides the qualities and reactions shown or described, our further action or analysis will call forth certain other groups of qualities and reactions constituting the *thing which is said to exist*. But aspects, in the case in which I have used that word, *are* what they are and do not necessarily imply anything beyond their own peculiarities. The words *true* or *false* can be applied to them only with the meaning of *aspects truly existing* or *not truly existing* ; *i.e.* aspects of which it is true or not to *say that they exist*. But as to an aspect being true or false in the sense of *misleading*, that question refers not to the *aspect* itself, but to the THING of which the aspect is taken as a part and a sign. Now the contemplation of the mere aspect, the beauty (or ugliness) of the aspect, does not itself necessitate or imply any such reference to a thing. Our contemplation of the beauty of a statue representing a Centaur may indeed be disturbed by the reflexion that a creature with two sets of lungs and digestive organs would be a monster and not likely to grow to the age of having a beard. But this disturbing thought need not take place. And when it takes place it is not part of our contemplation of the *aspect* of that statue; it is, on the contrary, outside it, an excursion away from it due to our inveterate (and very necessary) habit of interrupting the contemplation of *Aspects* by the thinking and testing of *Things*. The Aspect never implied the existence of a Thing beyond itself; it did not affirm that anything was true, *i.e.* that anything could or would happen besides the fact of our contemplation. In other words the formula that *beautiful is an adjective applying only to aspects*, shows us that art can be truthful or untruthful only in so far as art (as is often the case) deliberately sets to making statements about the existence and nature of Things. If Art says " Centaurs can be born and grow up to man's estate with two sets of respiratory and digestive organs "—then Art is telling lies. Only, before accusing it of being a liar, better make sure that the statement about the possibility of centaurs has been intended by the Art, and not merely read into it by ourselves.

But more of this when we come to the examination of Subject and Form.

CHAPTER IV

SENSATIONS

In the contemplation of the *Aspect* before him, what gave that æsthetic man the most immediate and undoubted pleasure was its colour, or, more correctly speaking, its colours. Psycho-Physiologists have not yet told us why colours, taken singly and apart from their juxtaposition, should possess so extraordinary a power over what used to be called our animal spirits, and through them over our moods ; and we can only guess from analogy with what is observed in plants, as well as from the nature of the phenomenon itself, that various kinds of luminous stimulation must have some deep chemical repercussion throughout the human organism. The same applies, though in lesser degree, to sounds, quite independent of their juxtaposition as melodies and harmonies. As there are colours which *feel*, *i.e.* make *us* feel, more or less warm or cool, colours which are refreshing or stifling, depressing or exhilarating quite independent of any associations, so also there are qualities of sound which enliven us like the blare of the trumpet, or harrow us like the quaver of the accordion.

Similarly with regard to immediacy of effect : the
first chords of an organ will change our whole mode
of being like the change of light and colour on first
entering a church, although the music which that
organ is playing may, after a few seconds of listening,
bore us beyond endurance ; and the architecture of
that church, once we begin to take stock of it,
entirely dispel that first impression made by the
church's light and colour. It is on account of this
doubtless physiological power of colour and sound,
this way which they have of invading and subjugat-
ing us with or without our consent and long before our
conscious co-operation, that the Man-on-the-Hill's
pleasure in the aspect before him was, as I have
said, first of all, pleasure in colour. Also, because
pleasure in colour, like pleasure in mere sound-
quality or *timbre*, is accessible to people who never
go any further in their æsthetic preference. Children,
as every one knows, are sensitive to colours,
long before they show the faintest sensitiveness for
shapes. And the timbre of a perfect voice in a
single long note or shake used to bring the house
down in the days of our grandparents, just as the
subtle orchestral blendings of Wagner entrance
hearers incapable of distinguishing the notes of a
chord and sometimes even incapable of following
a modulation.

The Man on the Hill, therefore, received immediate

pleasure from the colours of the landscape. *Received* pleasure, rather than *took* it, since colours, like smells, seem, as I have said, to invade us, and insist upon pleasing whether we want to be pleased or not. In this meaning of the word we may be said to be *passive* to sound and colour quality : our share in the effects of these sensations, as in the effect of agreeable temperatures, contacts and tastes, is a question of bodily and mental reflexes in which our conscious activity, our voluntary attention, play no part : we are not *doing*, but *done to* by those stimulations from without ; and the pleasure or displeasure which they set up in us is therefore one which we *receive*, as distinguished from one which *we take*.

Before passing on to the pleasure which the Man on the Hill *did take*, as distinguished from thus passively *receiving*, from the aspect before him, before investigating into the activities to which this other kind of pleasure, *pleasure taken, not received*, is due, we must dwell a little longer on the colours which delighted him, and upon the importance or unimportance of those colours with regard to that *Aspect* he was contemplating.

These colours — particularly a certain rain-washed blue, a pale lilac and a faded russet—gave him, as I said, immediate and massive pleasure like that of certain delicious tastes and smells,

indeed anyone who had watched him attentively
might have noticed that he was making rather the
same face as a person rolling, as Meredith says, a
fine vintage against his palate, or drawing in deeper
draughts of exquisitely scented air ; he himself, if
not too engaged in looking, might have noticed the
accompanying sensations in his mouth, throat and
nostrils ; all of which, his only active response to
the colour, was merely the attempt to *receive more*
of the already received sensation.   But this pleasure
which he received from the mere colours of the landscape was the same pleasure which they would have
given him if he had met them in so many skeins
of silk ; the more complex pleasure due to their
juxtaposition, was the pleasure he might have had
if those skeins, instead of being on separate leaves
of a pattern-book, had been lying tangled together
in an untidy work-basket.   He might then probably
have said, " Those are exactly the colours, and
in much the same combination, as in that landscape
we saw such and such a day, at such and such a
season and hour, from the top of that hill."   But
he would never have said (or been crazy if he had)
" Those skeins of silk ARE the landscape we saw in
that particular place and on that particular occasion."   Now the odd thing is that he would have
used that precise form of words, " that is the
landscape," etc. etc., if you had shown him a pencil

drawing or a photograph taken from that particular
place and point of view. And similarly if you had
made him look through stained glass which changed
the pale blue, pale lilac and faded russet into
emerald green and blood red. He would have
exclaimed at the loss of those exquisite colours
when you showed him the monochrome, and perhaps
have sworn that all his pleasure was spoilt when
you forced him to look through that atrocious glass.
But he would have identified the aspect as the one
he had seen before ; just as even the least musical
person would identify " God save the King " whether
played with three sharps on the flute or with four
flats on the trombone.

There is therefore in an *Aspect* something over
and above the quality of the colours (or in a piece
of music, of the sounds) in which that aspect is,
at any particular moment, embodied for your senses ;
something which can be detached from the particular
colours or sounds and re-embodied in other colours
or sounds, existing meanwhile in a curious potential
schematic condition in our memory. That something is *Shape*.

It is Shape which we contemplate ; and it is only
because they enter into shapes that colours and
sounds, as distinguished from temperatures, textures,
tastes and smells, can be said to be contemplated
at all. Indeed if we apply to single isolated colour-

or sound-qualities (that blue or russet, or the mere
timbre of a voice or an orchestra) the adjective
beautiful while we express our liking for smells,
tastes, temperatures and textures merely by the
adjectives *agreeable, delicious* ; this difference in our
speech is doubtless due to the fact that colours or
sounds are more often than not connected each
with other colours or other sounds into a Shape and
thereby become subject to contemplation more
frequently than temperatures, textures, smells and
tastes which cannot themselves be grouped into
shapes, and are therefore objects of contemplation
only when associated with colours and sounds, as
for instance, the smell of burning weeds in a description of autumnal sights, or the cool wetness of a
grotto in the perception of its darkness and its
murmur of waters.

On dismissing the practical and the scientific
man because they were *thinking away from aspects
to things*, I attempted to inventory the *aspect* in
whose contemplation their æsthetic companion had
remained absorbed. There were the colours, that
delicious recently-washed blue, that lilac and russet,
which gave the man his immediate shock of passive
and (as much as smell and taste) bodily pleasure.
But besides these my inventory contained another
kind of item : what I described as a fan-like arrangement of sharply convergent lines and an exquisitely

phrased sky-line of hills, picked up at rhythmical intervals into sharp crests and dropping down merely to rush up again in long rapid concave curves. And besides all this, there was the outline of a distant mountain, rising flamelike against the sky. It was all these items made up of *lines* (sky-line, outline, and lines of perspective!) which remained unchanged when the colours were utterly changed by looking through stained glass, and unchanged also when the colouring was reduced to the barest monochrome of a photograph or a pencil drawing; nay remained the same despite all changes of scale in that almost colourless presentment of them. Those items of the aspect were, as we all know, *Shapes*. And with altered colours, and colours diminished to just enough for each line to detach itself from its ground, those Shapes could be contemplated and called beautiful.

CHAPTER V

WHY should this be the case ? Briefly, because colours (and sounds) as such are forced upon us by external stimulation of our organs of sight and hearing, neither more nor less than various temperatures, textures, tastes and smells are forced upon us from without through the nervous and cerebral mechanism connected with our skin, muscle, palate and nose. Whereas shapes instead of being thus nilly willy *seen* or *heard*, are, at least until we know them, *looked* at or *listened* to, that is to say *taken in* or *grasped*, by mental and bodily activities which meet, but may also refuse to meet, those sense stimulations. Moreover, because these mental and bodily activities, being our own, can be rehearsed in what we call our memory without the repetition of the sensory stimulations which originally started them, and even in the presence of different ones.

In terms of mental science, colour and sound, like temperature, texture, taste and smell, are *sensations* ; while *shape* is, in the most complete sense, a *perception*. This distinction between *sensation* and *perception* is a technicality of psychology ;

but upon it rests the whole question why shapes can be contemplated and afford the satisfaction connected with the word *beautiful*, while colours and sounds, except as grouped or groupable into shapes, cannot. Moreover this distinction will prepare us for understanding the main fact of all psychological æsthetics : namely that the satisfaction or the dissatisfaction which we get from shapes is satisfaction or dissatisfaction in what are, directly or indirectly, activities of our own.

Etymologically and literally, *perception* means the act of *grasping* or *taking* in, and also the result of that action. But when we thus *perceive* a shape, what is it precisely that we grasp or take in ? At first it might seem to be the *sensations* in which that form is embodied. But a moment's reflection will show that this cannot be the case, since the sensations are furnished us simply without our performing any act of perception, thrust on us from outside, and, unless our sensory apparatus and its correlated brain centre were out of order, received by us passively, nilly willy, the Man on the Hill being invaded by the sense of that blue, that lilac and that russet exactly as he might have been invaded by the smell of the hay in the fields below. No : what we grasp or take in thus actively are not the sensations themselves, but the *relations* between these sensations, and it is of these relations, more truly than of the sensations themselves, that a shape is, in the most literal sense, *made up*. And it is this *making up of shapes*, this grasping or taking in of their constituent relations, which is an active process on our part, and one which we can either perform or not perform. When, instead of merely *seeing* a colour, we *look at* a shape, our eye ceases to be merely passive to the action of the various light-waves, and becomes active, and active in a more or less complicated way ; turning its differently sensitive portions to meet or avoid the stimulus, adjusting its focus like that of an opera glass, and like an opera glass, turning it to the right or left, higher or lower.

Moreover, except in dealing with very small surfaces, our eye moves about in our head and moves our head, and sometimes our whole body, along with it. An analogous active process undoubtedly distinguishes *listening* from mere *hearing* ; and although psycho-physiology seems still at a loss for the precise adjustments of the inner ear corresponding to the minute adjustments of the eye, it is generally recognised that auditive attention is accompanied by adjustments of the vocal parts, or preparations for such adjustments, which account for the impression of *following* a sequence of notes as we follow the appearance of colours and light, but as we do *not* follow, in the sense of *connecting*

by our activity, consecutive sensations of taste or
smell. Besides such obvious or presumable bodily
activities requisite for looking and listening as
distinguished from mere seeing and hearing, there
is moreover in all perception of shape, as in all
grasping of meaning, a mental activity involving
what are called *attention* and *memory*. A primer
of æsthetics is no place for expounding any of the
various psychological definitions of either of these,
let us call them, faculties. Besides I should prefer
that these pages deal only with such mental facts
as can be found in the Reader's everyday (however
unnoticed) experience, instead of requiring for their
detection the artificial conditions of specialised
introspection or laboratory experiment. So I shall
give to those much fought over words *attention*
and *memory* merely the rough and ready meaning
with which we are familiar in everyday language,
and only beg the Reader to notice that, whatever
psychologists may eventually prove or disprove
attention and *memory* to be, these two, let us un-
scientifically call them *faculties*, are what chiefly
distinguishes *perception* from *sensation*. For instance, in grasping or taking stock of a visible
or an audible shape we are doing something with
our attention, or our attention is doing something
in us : a travelling about, a returning to starting
points, a summing up. And a travelling about

not merely between what is given simultaneously
in the present, but, even more, between what has
been given in an immediately proximate past,
and what we expect to be given in an immediately
proximate future ; both of which, the past which
is put behind us as past, and the past which is
projected forwards as future, necessitate the activity
of *memory*. There is an adjustment of our feelings
as well as our muscles not merely to the present
sensation, but to the future one, and a buzz of continuing adjustment to the past.   There is a holding
over and a holding on, a reacting backwards and
forwards of our attention, and quite a little drama
of expectation, fulfilment and disappointment, or
as psychologists call them, of tensions and relaxa-
tions.   And this little drama involved in all looking or listening, particularly in all taking stock of
visible or audible (and I may add intellectual or
verbal) shape, has its appropriate accompaniment of
emotional changes : the ease or difficulty of understanding producing feelings of victory or defeat
which we shall deal with later.   And although the
various perceptive activities remain unnoticed in
themselves (so long as easy and uninterrupted),
we become aware of a lapse, a gap, whenever our
mind's eye (if not our bodily one !) neglects to sweep
from side to side of a geometrical figure, or from
centre to circumference, or again whenever our

C

mind's ear omits following from some particular note to another, just as when we fall asleep for a second during a lecture or sermon : we have, in common parlance, *missed the hang* of some detail or passage. What we have missed, in that lapse of attention, is a *relation*, the length and direction of a line, or the span of a musical interval, or, in the case of words, the references of noun and verb, the co-ordination of tenses of a verb. And it is such relations, more or less intricate and hierarchic, which transform what would otherwise be meaningless juxtapositions or sequences of sensations into the significant entities which can be remembered and recognised even when their constituent sensations are completely altered, namely *shapes*. To our previous formula that *beautiful* denotes satisfaction in contemplating an aspect, we can now add that an *aspect* consists of sensations grouped together into *relations* by our active, our remembering and foreseeing, perception.

CHAPTER VI

LET us now examine some of these relations, not in the genealogical or hierarchic order assigned to them by experimental psychology, but in so far as they constitute the elements of *shape*, and more especially as they illustrate the general principle which I want to impress on the Reader, namely : That the perception of Shape depends primarily upon movements which *we* make, and the measurements and comparisons which *we* institute.

And first we must examine mere *extension* as such, which distinguishes our active dealings with visual and audible sensations from our passive reception of the sensations of taste and smell. For while in the case of the latter a succession of similar stimulations affects us as " more taste of strawberry " or " more smell of rose " when intermittent, or as a vague " there *is* a strong or faint taste of strawberry " and a " there IS a smell of lemon flower "—when continuous ; our organ of sight being mobile, reports not " more black on white " but " so many inches of black line on a white ground," that is to say reports a certain *extension* answering to its own movement. This

quality of extension exists also in our sound-
perceptions, although the explanation is less evident.
Notes do not indeed exist (but only sounding bodies
and air-vibrations) in the space which we call
" real " because our eye and our locomotion coincide
in their accounts of it ; but notes are experienced,
that is thought and felt, as existing in a sort of imitation space of their own. This " musical space,"
as M. Dauriac has rightly called it, has limits corresponding with those of our power of hearing or
reproducing notes, and a central region corresponding with our habitual experience of the human
voice ; and in this " musical space " notes are
experienced as moving up and down and with a
centrifugal and centripetal direction, and also as
existing at definite spans or *intervals* from one
another ; all of which probably on account of
presumable muscular adjustments of the inner and
auditive apparatus, as well as obvious sensations
in the vocal parts when we ourselves produce, and
often when we merely think of, them. In visual
perception the sweep of the glance, that is the
adjustment of the muscles of the inner eye, the
outer eye and of the head, is susceptible of being
either interrupted or continuous like any other
muscular process ; and its continuity is what
unites the mere successive sensations of colour
and light into a unity of extension, so that the

same successive colour-and-light-sensations can be experienced either as *one* extension, or as two or more, according as the glance is continuous or interrupted ; the eye's sweep, when not excessive, tending to continuity *unless a new direction requires a new muscular adjustment.* And, except in the case of an *extension* exceeding any single movement of eye and head, a new adjustment answers to what we call *a change of direction. Extension* therefore, as we have forestalled with regard to sound, has various modes, corresponding to something belonging to ourselves : a *middle*, answering to the middle not of our field of vision, since that itself can be raised or lowered by a movement of the head, but to the middle of our body ; and an *above* and *below*, a *right* and a *left* referable to our body also, or rather to the adjustments made by eye and head in the attempt to see our own extremities ; for, as every primer of psychology will teach you, mere sight and its muscular adjustments account only for the dimensions of height (up and down) and of breadth (right and left) while the third or cubic dimension of *depth* is a highly complex result of locomotion in which I include prehension. And inasmuch as we are dealing with *aspects* and not with *things*, we have as yet nothing to do with this *cubic* or *third dimension*, but are confining ourselves to the two dimensions of extension in height and

breadth, which are sufficient for the existence, the
identity, or more correctly the *quiddity*, of visible
shapes.

Such a shape is therefore, primarily, a series of
longer or shorter *extensions*, given by a separate
glance towards, or away from, our own centre or
extremities, and at some definite angle to our own
axis and to the ground on which we stand. But
these acts of extension and orientation cease to be
thought of as measured and orientated, and indeed
as accomplished, by ourselves, and are translated
into objective terms whenever our attention is
turned outwards : thus we say that each line is of
a given length and direction, so or so much off the
horizontal or vertical.

So far we have established relations only to
ourselves. We now compare the acts of extension
one against the other, and we also measure the
adjustment requisite to pass from one to another,
continuing to refer them all to our own axis and
centre ; in everyday speech, we perceive that the
various lines are *similar* and *dissimilar* in length,
direction and orientation. We *compare* ; and comparing we *combine* them in the unity of our
intention : thought of together they are thought
of as belonging together. Meanwhile the process
of such comparison of the relation of each line
with us to the analogous relation to us of its

fellows, produces yet further acts of measurement and comparison. For in going from one of our lines to another we become aware of the presence of—how shall I express it ?—well of a *nothing* between them, what we call *blank space*, because we experience a *blank* of the particular sensations, say red and black, with which we are engaged in those lines. Between the red and black sensations of the lines we are looking at, there will be a possibility of other colour sensations, say the white of the paper, and these white sensations we shall duly receive, for, except by shutting our eyes, we could not avoid receiving them. But though received these white sensations will not be attended to, because they are not what we are busied with. We shall be *passive* towards the white sensations while we are *active* towards the black and red ones ; we shall not measure the white ; not sweep our glance along it as we do along the red and the black. And as *ceteris paribus* our tense awareness of active states always throws into insignificance a passive state sandwiched between them ; so, bent as we are upon our red and black extensions, and their comparative lengths and directions, we shall treat the uninteresting white extensions as a *blank*, a gap, as that which separates the objects of our active interest, and takes what existence it has for our mind only from its relation of separating those interesting actively measured and compared lines. Thus the difference between our *active perception* and our merely *passive sensation* accounts for the fact that every visible shape is composed of lines (or bands) measured and compared with reference to our own ocular adjustments and our axis and centre; lines existing, as we express it, in *blank space*, that is to say space not similarly measured; lines, moreover, *enclosing* between each other more of this blank space, which is not measured in itself but subjected to the measurement of its enclosing lines. And similarly, every *audible* Shape consists not merely of sounds enclosing *silence*, but of heard tones between which we are aware of the intervening *blank interval* which *might have been* occupied by the intermediary tones and semitones. In other words, visible and audible Shape is composed of alternations between *active*, that is *moving*, measuring, referring, comparing, attention; and *passive*, that is comparatively sluggish *reception* of mere sensation.

This fact implies another and very important one, which I have indeed already hinted at. If perceiving shape means comparing lines (they may *be bands*, but we will call them *lines*), and the lines are measured only by consecutive eye movements, then the act of comparison evidently includes the co-operation, however infinitesimally brief, of *memory*. The two halves of this chippendale chair-back exist simultaneously in front of my eyes, but I cannot take stock simultaneously of the lengths and orientation of the curves to the right and the curves of the left. I must hold over the image of one half, and unite it, somewhere in what we call " the mind "—with the other ; nay, I must do this even with the separate.curves constituting the patterns each of which is measured by a sweep of the glance, even as I should measure them successively by applying a tape and then remembering and comparing their various lengths, although the ocular process may stand to the tape-process as a minute of our time to several hundreds of years. This comes to saying that the perception of visible shapes, even like that of audible ones, takes place *in time*, and requires therefore the co-operation of *memory*. Now memory, paradoxical as it may sound, practically implies *expectation* : the use of the past, to so speak, is to become that visionary thing we call the *future*. Hence, while we are measuring the extension and direction of one line, we are not only *remembering* the extent and direction of another previously measured line, but we are also *expecting* a similar, or somewhat similar, act of measurement of the *next* line ; even as in " following a melody " we not only remember the preceding tone, but *expect* the succeeding ones. Such interplay of present, past and future is requisite for every kind of *meaning*, for every *unit of thought*; and among others, of the meaning, the *thought*, which we contemplate under the name of *shape*. It is on account of this interplay of present, past and future, that Wundt counts feelings *of tension* and *relaxation* among the *elements* of form-perception. And the mention of such *feelings*, i.e. rudiments of *emotion*, brings us to recognise that the remembering and foreseeing of our acts of measurement and orientation constitutes a microscopic psychological drama—shall we call it the drama of the SOUL MOLECULES ?—whose first familiar examples are those two peculiarities of visible and audible shape called *Symmetry* and *Rythm*.

Both of these mean that a measurement has been made, and that the degree of its *span* is kept in memory to the extent of our expecting that the next act of measurement will be similar. *Symmetry* exists quite as much in *Time* (hence in shapes made up of sound-relations) as in *Space*; and *Rythm*, which is commonly thought of as an especially musical relation, exists as much in *Space* as in *Time*; because the perception of shape requires Time and movement equally whether the relations are between objectively co-existent and durable marks on stone or paper, or between objectively successive and fleeting sound-waves. Also because, while the single relations of lines and of sounds require to be ascertained successively, the combination of those various single relations, their relations with one another *as whole and parts*, require to be grasped by an intellectual synthesis ; as much in the case of notes as in the case of lines.   If, in either case, we did not remember the first measurement when we obtained the second, there would be no perception of shape however elementary ; which is the same as saying that for an utterly oblivious mind there could be no relationships, and therefore no meaning.   In the case of Symmetry the relations are not merely the lengths and directions of the single lines, that is to say their relations to ourselves, and the relation established by comparison between these single lines ; there is now also the relation of both to a third, itself of course related to ourselves, indeed, as regards visible shape, usually answering to our own axis.   The expectation which is liable to fulfilling or balking is therefore that of a repetition of this double relationship remembered between the lengths and directions on one side, by the lengths and directions on the other ; and the repetition of a common relation to a central item.

The case of RYTHM is more complex.   For, although we usually think of Rythm as a relation of *two* items, it is in reality a relation of four (or more); because what we remember and expect is a mixture of similarity with dissimilarity between lengths, directions or impacts. OR IMPACTS. For with Rythm we come to another point illustrative of the fact that all shape-elements depend upon our own activity and its modes. A rythmical arrangement is not necessarily one between *objectively* alternated elements like objectively longer or shorter lines of a pattern, or *objectively* higher or lower or longer and shorter notes. Rythm exists equally where the objective data, the sense stimulations, are uniform, as is the case with the ticks of a clock. These ticks would be registered as exactly similar by appropriate instruments. But our mind is not such an impassive instrument : our mind (whatever our mind may really be) is subject to an alternation of *more* and *less*, of *vivid* and *less vivid*, *important* and *less important*, of *strong* and *weak* ; and the objectively similar stimulations from outside, of sound or colour or light, are perceived as vivid or less vivid, important or less important, according to the beat of this mutual alternation with which they coincide : thus the uniform ticking of the clock will be perceived by us as a succession in which the stress, that is the importance, is thrown upon the first or the second member of a group ; and the recollection and expectation are therefore of a unity of dissimilar importance. We hear STRONG-WEAK ; and remembering *strong-weak,* we make a new *strong-weak* out of that objective uniformity.

Here there is no objective reason for one rythm more than another ; and we express this by saying that the tickings of a clock have no intrinsic form. For *Form*, or as I prefer to call it, *Shape*, although it exists only in the mind capable of establishing and correlating its constituent relationships, takes an objective existence when the material stimulations from the outer world are such as to force all normally constituted minds to the same series and combinations of perceptive acts ; a fact which explains why the artist can transmit the shapes existing in his own mind to the mind of a beholder or hearer by combining certain objective stimulations, say those of pigments on paper or of sound vibrations in time, so as to provoke perceptive activities similar to those which would, *ceteris paribus,* have been provoked in himself if that shape had not existed first of all *only* in his mind.

A further illustration of the principle that shape-perception is a combination of active measurements and comparisons, and of remembrance and expectations, is found in a fact which has very great importance in all artistic dealings with shapes. I have spoken, for simplicity's, sake, as if the patches of colour on a blank (i.e. uninteresting) ground along which the glance sweeps, were invariably contiguous and continuous. But these colour patches, and the sensations they afford us, are just as often,

discontinuous in the highest degree ; and the lines
constituting a shape may, as for instance in constellations, be entirely imaginary. The fact is that
what we feel as a line is not an objective continuity
of colour-or-light-patches, but the continuity of our
glance's sweep which may either accompany this
objective continuity or replace it. Indeed such
imaginary lines thus established between isolated
colour patches, are sometimes felt as more vividly
existing than real ones, because the glance is not
obliged to take stock of their parts, but can rush
freely from extreme point to extreme point. Moreover not only half the effectiveness of design, but
more than half the efficiency of practical life, is
due to our establishing such imaginary lines. We
are inevitably and perpetually dividing visual space
(and something of the sort happens also with
" musical space ") by objectively non-existent lines
answering to our own bodily orientation. Every
course, every trajectory, is of this sort. And every
drawing executed by an artist, every landscape,
offered us by " Nature," is felt, because it is measured,
with reference to a set of imaginary horizontals or
perpendiculars. While, as I remember the late
Mr G. F. Watts showing me, every curve which we
look at is *felt as being* part of an imaginary circle
into which it could be prolonged. Our sum of
measuring and comparing activities, and also our

dramas of remembrance and expectation, are therefore multiplied by these imaginary lines, whether they connect, constellation-wise, a few isolated colour indications, or whether they are established as standards of reference (horizontals, verticals, etc.) for other really existing lines ; or whether again they be thought of, like those circles, as *wholes* of which objectively perceived series of colour patches might possibly be *parts*. In all these cases imaginary lines are *felt*, as existing, inasmuch as we feel the movement by which we bring them into existence, and even feel that such a movement might be made by us when it is not.

So far, however, I have dealt with these imaginary lines only as an additional proof that shape-perception is an establishment of two dimensional relationships, through our own activities, and an active remembering, foreseeing and combining thereof.

CHAPTER VII

FACILITY AND DIFFICULTY OF GRASPING

OF this we get further proof when we proceed to another and less elementary relationship implied in the perception of shape : the relation of Whole and Parts.

In dealing with the *ground* upon which we perceive our red and black patches to be extended, I have already pointed out that our operations of measuring and comparing are not applied to all the patches of colour which we actually see, but only to such as we *look at*; an observation equally applicable to sounds. In other words our attention selects certain sensations, and limits to these all that establishing of relations, all that measuring and comparing, all that remembering and expecting ; the other sensations being excluded. Now, while whatever is thus merely seen, but not looked at, is excluded as so much *blank* or *otherness* ; whatever is, on the contrary, *included* is thereby credited with the quality of belonging, that is to say being included, together. And the more the attention alternates between the measuring of *included* extensions and directions and the expectation of equivalent (symmetrical

48

or rythmical) extensions or directions or stresses, the closer will become the relation of these items *included* by our attention and the more foreign will become the *excluded otherness* from which, as we feel, they *detach themselves*. But—by an amusing paradox—these lines measured and compared by our attention, are themselves not only *excluding* so much *otherness or blank* ; they also tend, so soon as referred to one another, to *include* some of this uninteresting blankness ; and it is across this more or less completely included blankness that the eye (and the imagination !) draw such imaginary lines as I have pointed out with reference to the constellations. Thus a circle, say of red patches, *excludes* some of the white paper on which it is drawn ; but it *includes* or *encloses* the rest. Place a red patch somewhere on that *enclosed* blank ; our glance and attention will now play not merely along the red circumference, but to and fro between the red circumference and the red patch, thereby establishing imaginary but thoroughly measured and compared lines between the two. Draw a red line from the red patch to the red circumference ; you will begin expecting similar lengths on the other sides of the red patch, and you will become aware that these imaginary lines are, or are not, equal ; in other words, that the red patch is, or is not, equidistant from every point of the red circum-

D

ference. And if the red patch is not thus in the middle, you will expect, and imagine another patch which *is*; and from this *imaginary centre* you will draw imaginary lines, that is you will make by no means imaginary glance-sweeps, to the red circumference. Thus you may go on adding real red lines and imaginary lines connecting them with the circumference; and the more you do so the more you will feel that all these real lines and imaginary lines and all the blank space which the latter measure, are connected, or susceptible of being connected, closer and closer, every occasional excursion beyond the boundary only bringing you back with an increased feeling of this interconnexion, and an increased expectation of realising it in further details. But if on one of these glance-flickings beyond the circumference, your attention is caught by some colour patch or series of colour patches outside of it, you will either cease being interested in the circle and wander away to the new colour patches; or more probably, try to connect that outlying colour with the circle and its radii; or again failing that, you will " overlook it," as, in a pattern of concentric circles you overlook a colour band which, as you express it " has nothing to do with it," that is with what you are looking at. Or again listening to. For if a church-bell mixes its tones and rythm with that of a symphony you are listening to, you may try and bring them in, make a place for them, *expect* them among the other tones or rythms. Failing which you will, after a second or two, cease to notice those bells, cease to listen to them, giving all your attention once more to the sonorous whole whence you have expelled those intruders ; or else, again, the intrusion will become an interruption, and the bells, once *listened to*, will prevent your listening adequately to the symphony.

Moreover, if the number of extensions, directions, real or imaginary lines or musical intervals, alternations of *something* and *nothing*, prove too great for your powers of measurement and comparison, particularly if it all surpass your habitual interplay of recollection and expectation, you will say (as before an over intricate pattern or a piece of music of unfamiliar harmonies and rythm) that " you can't grasp it "—that you " miss the hang of it." And what you will feel is that you cannot keep the parts within the whole, that the boundary vanishes, that what has been included unites with the excluded, in fact that all *shape* welters into chaos. And as if to prove once more the truth of our general principle, you will have a hateful feeling of having been trifled with. What has been balked and wasted are all your various activities of measuring, comparing and co-ordinating ; what has been trifled with are your expectations. And so far from contemplating with satisfaction the objective cause of all this vexation and disappointment, you will avoid contemplating it at all, and explain your avoidance by calling that chaotic or futile assemblage of lines or of notes " ugly."

We seem thus to have got a good way in our explanation; and indeed the older psychology, for instance of the late Grant Allen, did not get any further. But to explain why a shape difficult to perceive should be disliked and called " ugly," by no means amounts to explaining why some other shape should be liked and called " beautiful," particularly as some ugly shapes happen to be far easier to grasp than some beautiful ones. The Reader will indeed remember that there is a special pleasure attached to all overcoming of difficulty, and to all understanding. But this double pleasure is shared with form-perception by every other successful grasping of meaning; and there is no reason why that pleasure should be repeated in the one case more than in the other; nor why we should repeat looking at (which is what we mean by contemplating) a shape once we have grasped it, any more than we continue to dwell on, to reiterate the mental processes by which we have worked out a geometrical proposition or unravelled a metaphysical crux. The sense of victory ends very soon after the sense of the difficulty overcome; the sense of illumination ends with the acquisition of a piece of information ; and we pass on to some new obstacle and some new riddle. But it is different in the case of what we call *Beautiful*. *Beautiful* means satisfactory for contemplation, *i.e.* for reiterated perception ; and the very essence of contemplative satisfaction is its desire for such reiteration. The older psychology would perhaps have explained this reiterative tendency by the pleasurableness of the sensory elements, the mere colours and sounds of which the easily perceived shape is made up. But this does not explain why, given that other shapes are made up of equally agreeable sensory elements, we should not pass on from a once perceived shape or combination of shapes to a new one, thus obtaining, in addition to the sensory agreeableness of colour or sound, a constantly new output of that feeling of victory and illumination attendant on every successful intellectual effort. Or, in other words, seeing that painting and music employ sensory elements already selected as agreeable, we ought never to wish to see the same picture twice, or to continue looking at it ; we ought never to wish to repeat the same piece of music or its separate phrases ; still less to cherish that picture or piece of music in our memory, going over and over again as much of its shape as had become our permanent possession.

We return therefore to the fact that although balked perception is enough to make us reject a shape as *ugly*, *i.e.* such that we avoid entering into contemplation of it, easy perception is by no means sufficient to make us cherish a shape *as beautiful*, *i.e.* such that the reiteration of our drama of perception becomes desirable. And we shall have to examine whether there may not be some other factor of shape-perception wherewith to account for this preference of reiterated looking at the same to looking at something else.

Meanwhile we may add to our set of formulæ : difficulty in shape-perception makes contemplation disagreeable and impossible, and hence earns for aspects the adjective *ugly*. But facility in perception, like agreeableness of sensation by no means suffices for satisfied contemplation, and hence for the use of the adjective Beautiful.

CHAPTER VIII

SUBJECT AND OBJECT

But before proceeding to this additional factor in shape-perception, namely that of Empathic Interpretation, I require to forestall an objection which my Reader has doubtless been making throughout my last chapters ; more particularly that in clearing away the ground of this objection I shall be able to lay the foundations of my further edifice of explanation. The objection is this : if the man on the hill was aware of performing any, let alone all, of the various operations described as constituting shape-perception, neither that man nor any other human being would be able to enjoy the shapes thus perceived.

My answer is :

When did I say or imply that he was *aware* of doing any of it ? It is not only possible, but extremely common, to perform processes without being aware of performing them. The man was not *aware*, for instance, of making eye adjustments and eye movements, unless indeed his sight was out of order. Yet his eye movements could have been cinematographed, and his eye adjustments have been

described minutely in a dozen treatises. He was
no more aware of *doing* any measuring or comparing
than we are aware of *doing* our digestion or circula-
tion, except when we do them badly. But just as we
are aware of our digestive and circulatory processes
in the sense of being aware of the animal spirits
resulting from their adequate performance, so he
was aware of his measuring and comparing, inasmuch
as he was aware that the line A—B was longer than
the line C—D, or that the point E was half an inch
to the left of the point F. For so long as we are
neither examining into ourselves, nor called upon to
make a choice between two possible proceedings,
nor forced to do or suffer something difficult or
distressing, in fact so long as we are attending to
whatever absorbs our attention and not to our
processes of attending, those processes are replaced
in our awareness by the very facts—for instance
the proportions and relations of lines—resulting
from their activity. That these results should not
resemble their cause, that mental elements (as they
are called) should appear and disappear, and also
combine into unaccountable compounds (Browning's
" not a third sound, but a star ") according as we
attend to them, is indeed the besetting difficulty
of a science carried on by the very processes which
it studies. But it is so because it is one of Psychology's basic facts. And, so far as we are at

present concerned, this difference between mental processes and their results is the fact upon which psychological æsthetics are based. And it is not in order to convert the Man on the Hill to belief in his own acts of shape-perception, nor even to explain why he was not aware of them, that I am insisting upon this point. The principle I have been expounding, let us call it that of the *merging of the perceptive activities of the subject in the qualities of the object of perception*, explains another and quite as important mental process which was going on in that unsuspecting man.

But before proceeding to that I must make it clearer how that man stood in the matter of *awareness of himself*. He was, indeed, aware of himself whenever, during his contemplation of that landscape, the thought arose, " well, I must be going away, and perhaps I shan't see this place again "—or some infinitely abbreviated form, perhaps a mere sketched out gesture of turning away, accompanied by a slight feeling of *clinging*, he couldn't for the life of him say in what part of his body. He was at that moment acutely aware that he *did not want* to do something which it was optional to do. Or, if he acquiesced passively in the necessity of going away, aware that he *wanted to come back*, or at all events wanted to carry off as much as possible of what he had seen. In short he was aware of himself either making the effort of tearing himself away, or, if some other person or mere habit, saved him this effort, he was aware of himself making another effort to impress that landscape on his memory, and aware of a future self making an effort to return to it. I call it *effort*; you may, if you prefer, call it WILL; at all events the man was aware of himself as nominative of a verb to *cling to*, (in the future tense) *return to*, to *choose as against some other alternative*; as nominative of a verb briefly, *to like* or *love*. And the accusative of these verbs would be the landscape. But unless the man's contemplation was thus shot with similar ideas of some action or choice of his own, he would express the situation by saying "this landscape *is* awfully beautiful."

This IS. I want you to notice the formula, by which the landscape, ceasing to be the accusative of the man's looking and thinking, becomes the nominative of a verb *to be so-and-so*. That grammatical transformation is the sign of what I have designated, in philosophical language, *as the merging of the activities of the subject in the object*. It takes place already in the domain of simple sensation whenever, instead of saying "*I* taste or *I* smell something nice or nasty" we say—"*this thing* tastes or smells nice or nasty." And I have now shown you how this tendency to put the cart before

the horse increases when we pass to the more complex and active processes called perception ; turning
" I measure this line "—" I compare these two
angles " into " this line *extends* from A to B "
—" these two angles *are equal* to two right
angles."

But before getting to the final inversion—" this
landscape *is* beautiful " instead of " *I* like this
landscape "—there is yet another, and far more
curious merging of the subject's activities in the
qualities of the object. This further putting of the
cart before the horse (and, you will see, attributing
to the cart what only the horse can be doing !) falls
under the head of what German psychologists call
Einfühlung, or " Infeeling "—which Prof. Titchener
has translated *Empathy*. Now this new, and comparatively newly discovered element in our perception of shape is the one to which, leaving out of
account the pleasantness of mere colour and sound
sensations as such, we probably owe the bulk of
whatever satisfaction we connect with the word
Beautiful. And I have already given the Reader
an example of such Empathy when I described
the landscape seen by the man on the hill as
consisting of a skyline " *dropping down merely
to rush up again in rapid concave curves* " ; to
which I might have added that there was also a
plain which *extended*, a valley which *wound along*,

paths which *climbed* and roads which *followed* the *undulations* of the land. But the best example was when I said that opposite to the man there was a distant mountain *rising* against the sky.

CHAPTER IX

THE mountain rises. What do we mean when we employ this form of words ? Some mountains, we are told, have originated in an *upheaval*. But even if this particular mountain did, we never saw it and geologists are still disputing about HOW and WHETHER. So the *rising* we are talking about is evidently not that probable or improbable *upheaval*. On the other hand all geologists tell us that every mountain is undergoing a steady *lowering* through its particles being weathered away and washed down ; and our knowledge of landslips and avalanches shows us that the mountain, so far from rising, is *descending*. Of course we all know that, objects the Reader, and of course nobody imagines that the rock and the earth of the mountain is rising, or that the mountain is getting up or growing taller ! All we mean is that the mountain *looks* as if it were rising.

The mountain *looks !* Surely here is a case of putting the cart before the horse. No ; we cannot explain the mountain *rising* by the mountain *looking*, for the only *looking* in the business is *our* looking *at* the mountain. And if the Reader objects again that these are all *figures of speech*, I shall answer that *Empathy* is what explains why we employ figures of speech at all, and occasionally employ them, as in the case of this rising mountain, when we know perfectly well that the figure we have chosen expresses the exact reverse of the objective truth. Very well ; then, (says the Reader) we will avoid all figures of speech and say merely : when we look at the mountain *we somehow or other think of the action of rising*. Is that sufficiently literal and indisputable ?

So literal and indisputable a statement of the case, I answer, that it explains, when we come to examine it, why we have said that the mountain rises. For if the Reader remembers my chapter on shape-perception, he will have no difficulty in answering why we should have a thought of rising when we look at the mountain, since we cannot look at the mountain, nor at a tree, a tower or anything of which we similarly say that it *rises*, without lifting our glance, raising our eye and probably raising our head and neck, all of which raising and lifting unites into a general awareness of something *rising*. The rising of which we are aware is going on in us. But, as the Reader will remember also, when we are engrossed by something outside ourselves, as we are engrossed in looking at the shape (for we can *look* at only the shape, not the *substance*) of that mountain we cease thinking about ourselves, and cease thinking about ourselves exactly in proportion as we are thinking of the mountain's shape. What becomes therefore of our awareness of raising or lifting or *rising* ? What can become of it (so long as it continues to be there !) except that it coalesces with the shape we are looking at ; in short that the *rising* continuing to be thought, but no longer to be thought of with reference to ourselves (since we aren't thinking of ourselves), is thought of in reference to what we *are* thinking about, namely the mountain, or rather the mountain's shape, which is, so to speak, responsible for any thought of rising, since it obliges us to lift, raise or rise ourselves in order to take stock of it. It is a case exactly analogous to our transferring the measuring done by our eye to the line of which we say that it *extends* from A to B, when in reality the only *extending* has been the extending of our glance. It is a case of what I have called the tendency to merge the *activities* of the perceiving subject with the qualities of the perceived object. Indeed if I insisted so much upon this tendency of our mind, I did so largely because of its being at the bottom of the phenomenon of *Empathy*, as we have just seen it exemplified in the *mountain which rises*.

If this is Empathy, says the Reader (relieved and

reassured), am I to understand that Empathy is nothing beyond *attributing what goes on in us when we look at a shape to the shape itself ?*

I am sorry that the matter is by no means so simple ! If what we attributed to each single shape was only the precise action which we happen to be accomplishing in the process of looking at it, Empathy would indeed be a simple business, but it would also be a comparatively poor one. No. The *rising* of the mountain is an idea started by the awareness of our own lifting or raising of our eyes, head or neck, and it is an idea containing the awareness of that lifting or raising. But it is far more than the idea merely of that lifting or raising which we are doing at this particular present moment and in connexion with this particular mountain. That present and particular raising and lifting is merely the nucleus to which gravitates our remembrance of all similar acts of raising, or *rising* which we have ever accomplished or seen accomplished, *raising* or *rising* not only of our eyes and head, but of every other part of our body, and of every part of every other body which we ever perceived to be rising. And not merely the thought of past *rising* but the thought also of future rising. All these risings, done by ourselves or watched in others, actually experienced or merely imagined, have long since united together in our mind, con-

stituting a sort of composite photograph whence
all differences are eliminated and wherein all
similarities are fused and intensified : the general
idea of *rising*, not " I rise, rose, will rise, it rises,
has risen or will rise" but merely *rising as* such,
rising as it is expressed not in any particular tense
or person of the verb *to rise*, but in that verb's
infinitive. It is this universally applicable notion
of rising, which is started in our mind by the awareness of the particular present acts of raising or
rising involved in our looking at that mountain,
and it is this general idea of rising, *i.e.* of *upward
movement*, which gets transferred to the mountain
along with our own particular present activity of
raising some part of us, and which thickens and
enriches and marks that poor little thought of a
definite raising with the interest, the emotional
fullness gathered and stored up in its long manifold
existence. In other words : what we are transferring (owing to that tendency to merge the
activities of the perceiving subject with the qualities
of the perceived object) from ourselves to the
looked at shape of the mountain, is not merely the
thought of the rising which is really being done
by us at that moment, but the thought and emotion,
the *idea of rising as such* which had been accumulat-
ing in our mind long before we ever came into the
presence of that particular mountain. And it is

E

this complex mental process, by which we (all unsuspectingly) invest that inert mountain, that bodiless shape, with the stored up and averaged and essential modes of our activity—it is this process whereby we make the mountain *raise itself*, which constitutes what, accepting Prof. Titchener's translation [1] of the German word *Einfühlung*, I have called Empathy.

The German word *Einfühlung* " feeling into "— derived from a *verb to feel oneself into something* (" sich in Etwas ein fühlen ") was in current use even before Lotze and Vischer applied it to æsthetics, and some years before Lipps (1897) and Wundt (1903) adopted it into psychological terminology ; and as it is now consecrated, and no better occurs to me, I have had to adopt it, although the literal connotations of the German word have surrounded its central meaning (as I have just defined it) with several mischievous misinterpretations. Against two of these I think it worth while to warn the Reader, especially as, while so doing, I can, in showing what it is not, make it even clearer what Empathy really is. The first of these two main misinterpretations is based upon the reflexive form of the German verb " *sich einfühlen* " (to feel *oneself* into) and it defines, or rather does not define, Empathy as a metaphysical and quasi-mythological

[1] From ἐν and πάσχω, ἔπαθον.

projection of the ego into the object or shape under observation ; a notion incompatible with the fact that Empathy, being only another of those various mergings of the activities of the perceiving subject with the qualities of the perceived object wherewith we have already dealt, depends upon a comparative or momentary abeyance of all thought of an ego ; if we became aware that it is *we* who are thinking the rising, we who are *feeling* the rising, we should not think or feel that the mountain did the rising. The other (and as we shall later see) more justifiable misinterpretation of the word Empathy is based on its analogy with *sympathy*, and turns it into a kind of sympathetic, or as it has been called, *inner, i.e.* merely *felt, mimicry* of, for instance, the mountain's *rising*. Such mimicry, not only *inner* and *felt*, but outwardly manifold, does undoubtedly often result from very lively *empathic* imagination. But as it is the mimicking, inner or outer, of movements and actions which, like the *rising* of the mountain, take place only in our imagination, it presupposes such previous animation of the inanimate, and cannot therefore be taken either as constituting or explaining Empathy itself.

Such as I have defined and exemplified it in our Rising Mountain, Empathy is, together with mere Sensation, probably the chief factor of preference, that is of an alternative of satisfaction and dissatisfaction, in æsthetic contemplation, the muscular adjustments and the measuring, comparing and co-ordinating activities by which Empathy is started, being indeed occasionally difficult and distressing, but giving in themselves little more than a negative satisfaction, at the most that of difficulty overcome and suspense relieved. But although nowhere so fostered as in the contemplation of shapes, Empathy exists or tends to exist throughout our mental life. It is, indeed, one of our simpler, though far from absolutely elementary, psychological processes, entering into what is called imagination, sympathy, and also into that inference from our own inner experience which has shaped all our conceptions of an outer world, and given to the intermittent and heterogeneous sensations received from without the framework of our constant and highly unified inner experience, that is to say, of our own activities and aims. Empathy can be traced in all of modes of speech and thought, particularly in the universal attribution of *doing* and *having* and *tending* where all we can really assert is successive and varied *being*. Science has indeed explained away the anthropomorphic implications of *Force* and *Energy*, *Attraction* and *Repulsion*; and philosophy has reduced *Cause* and *Effect* from implying intention and effort to meaning mere constant succession. But Empathy still helps us to many valuable ana-

logies ; and it is possible that without its constantly
checked but constantly renewed action, human
thought would be without logical cogency, as it
certainly would be without poetical charm.   Indeed
if Empathy is so recent a discovery, this may be
due to its being part and parcel of our thinking ;
so that we are surprised to learn its existence, as
Molière's good man was to hear that he talked
prose.

CHAPTER X

THE MOVEMENT OF LINES

ANY tendency to Empathy is perpetually being checked by the need for practical thinking. We are made to think in the most summary fashion from one to another of those grouped possibilities, past, present and future, which we call a Thing ; and in such discursive thinking we not only leave far behind the *aspect*, the shape, which has started a given scheme of Empathy, a given *movement of lines*, but we are often faced by facts which utterly contradict it. When, instead of looking at a particular *aspect* of that mountain, we set to climbing it ourselves, the mountain ceases to " rise " ; it becomes passive to the activity which our muscular sensations and our difficulty of breathing locate most unmistakably in ourselves. Besides which, in thus dealing with the mountain as a *thing*, we are presented with a series of totally different aspects or shapes, some of which suggest empathic activities totally different from that of rising. And the mountain in question, seen from one double its height, will suggest the empathic activity of *spreading itself out*. Moreover practical life hustles us into a succession of more

and more summary perceptions ; we do not actually
see more than is necessary for the bare recognition
of whatever we are dealing with and the adjustment
of our actions not so much to what it already is, as
to what it is likely to become. And this which is
true of seeing with the bodily eye, is even more
so of seeing, or rather *not* seeing but *recognising*,
with the eye of the spirit. The practical man on
the hill, and his scientific companion, (who is merely,
so to speak, a man *unpractically* concerned with
practical causes and changes) do not thoroughly see
the shapes of the landscape before them ; and still
less do they see the precise shape of the funiculars,
tramways, offices, cheques, volcanoes, ice-caps and
prehistoric inhabitants of their thoughts. There is
not much chance of Empathy and Empathy's
pleasures and pains in their lightning-speed, touch-
and-go visions !

    But now let us put ourselves in the place of their
æsthetically contemplative fellow-traveller. And,
for simplicity's sake, let us imagine him contemplating more especially one shape in that landscape,
the shape of that distant mountain, the one whose
" rising "—came to an end as soon as we set to
climbing it. The mountain is so far off that its
detail is entirely lost ; all we can see is a narrow
and pointed cone, perhaps a little *toppling* to one
side, of uniform hyacinth blue *detaching* itself from

the clear evening sky, into which, from the paler misty blue of the plain, it *rises*, a mere bodiless shape. It *rises*. There is at present no doubt about its *rising*. It rises and keeps on rising, never stopping unless *we* stop looking at it. It rises and never *has* risen. Its drama of two lines *striving* (one with more suddenness of energy and purpose than the other) to *arrive* at a particular imaginary point in the sky, *arresting* each other's *progress* as they *meet* in their *endeavour*, this simplest empathic action of an irregular and by no means rectilinear triangle, goes on repeating itself, like the parabola of a steadily spirting fountain : for ever accomplishing itself anew and for ever accompanied by the same effect on the feelings of the beholder.

It is this reiterative nature which, joined to its schematic definiteness, gives Empathy its extraordinary power over us. Empathy, as I have tried to make clear to the Reader, is due not only to the movements which we are actually making in the course of shape-perception, to present movements with their various modes of speed, intensity and facility and their accompanying intentions ; it is due at least as much to our accumulated and averaged past experience of movements of the same kind, also with *their* cognate various modes of speed, intensity, facility, and *their* accompanying intentions. And being thus residual averaged, and essential,

this empathic movement, this movement attributed
to the lines of a shape, is not clogged and inhibited
by whatever clogs and inhibits each separate concrete
experience of the kind ; still less is it overshadowed
in our awareness by the *result* which we foresee as
goal of our real active proceedings. For unless
they involve bodily or mental strain, our real and
therefore transient movements do not affect us as
pleasant or unpleasant, because our attention is
always outrunning them to some momentary goal ;
and the faint awareness of them is usually mixed
up with other items, sensations and perceptions,
of wholly different characters. Thus, in themselves
and apart from their aims, our bodily movements
are never interesting except inasmuch as requiring
new and difficult adjustments, or again as producing
perceptible repercussions in our circulatory, breathing and balancing apparatus : a waltz, or a dive
or a gallop may indeed be highly exciting, thanks
to its resultant organic perturbations and its concomitants of overcome difficulty and danger, but
even a dancing dervish's intoxicating rotations
cannot afford him much of the specific interest of
movement as movement. Yet every movement
which we accomplish implies a change in our debit
and credit of vital economy, a change in our balance
of bodily and mental expenditure and replenish-
ment ; and this, if brought to our awareness, is not

only interesting, but interesting in the sense either of pleasure or displeasure, since it implies the more or less furtherance or hindrance of our life-processes. Now it is this complete awareness, this brimfull interest in our own dynamic changes, in our various and variously combined facts of movement inasmuch as *energy* and *intention*, it is this sense of the *values of movement* which Empathy, by its schematic simplicity and its reiteration, is able to reinstate. The contemplation, that is to say the *isolating and reiterating perception*, of shapes and in so far of the qualities and relations of movement which Empathy invests them with, therefore shields our dynamic sense from all competing interests, clears it from all varying and irrelevant concomitants, gives it, as Faust would have done to the instant of happiness, a sufficient duration ; and reinstating it in the centre of our consciousness, allows it to add the utmost it can to our satisfaction or dissatisfaction

Hence the mysterious importance, the attraction or repulsion, possessed by shapes, audible as well as visible, according to their empathic character ; movement and energy, all that we feel as being life, is furnished by them in its essence and allowed to fill our consciousness. This fact explains also another phenomenon, which in its turn greatly adds to the power of that very Empathy of which it is a result. I am speaking once more of that phenomenon called *Inner Mimicry* which certain observers, themselves highly subject to it, have indeed considered as Empathy's explanation, rather than its result. In the light of all I have said about the latter, it becomes intelligible that when empathic imagination (itself varying from individual to individual) happens to be united to a high degree of (also individually very varying) muscular responsiveness, there may be set up reactions, actual or incipient, *e.g.* alterations of bodily attitude or muscular tension which (unless indeed they withdraw attention from the contemplated object to our own body) will necessarily add to the sum of activity empathically attributed to the contemplated object. There are moreover individuals in whom such " mimetic " accompaniment consists (as is so frequently the case in listening to music) in changes of the bodily balance, the breathing and heart-beats, in which cases additional doses of satisfaction or dissatisfaction result from the participation of bodily functions themselves so provocative of comfort or discomfort. Now it is obvious that such mimetic accompaniments, and every other associative repercussion into the seat of what our fathers correctly called " animal spirits," would be impossible unless reiteration, the reiteration of repeated acts of attention, had allowed the various empathic significance, the various *dynamic values*, of given shapes to sink so deeply into us, to become so habitual, that even a rapid glance (as when we perceive the upspringing lines of a mountain from the window of an express train) may suffice to evoke their familiar dynamic associations. Thus contemplation explains, so to speak, why contemplation may be so brief as to seem no contemplation at all : past repetition has made present repetition unnecessary, and the empathic, the dynamic scheme of any particular shape may go on working long after the eye is fixed on something else, or be started by what is scarcely a perception at all ; we feel joy at the mere foot-fall of some beloved person, but we do so because he is already beloved. Thus does the reiterative character essential to Empathy explain how our contemplative satisfaction in shapes, our pleasure in the variously combined *movements of lines*, irradiates even the most practical, the apparently least contemplative, moments and occupations of our existence.

But this is not all. This reiterative character of Empathy, this fact that the mountain is always rising without ever beginning to sink or adding a single cubit to its stature, joined to the abstract (the *infinitive of the verb*) nature of the suggested activity, together account for art's high impersonality and its existing, in a manner, *sub specie aeternitatis*. The drama of lines and curves presented

by the humblest design on bowl or mat partakes
indeed of the strange immortality of the youths
and maidens on the *Grecian Urn*, to whom Keats,
as you remember, says :—

> " Fond lover, never, never canst thou kiss,
>   Though winning near the goal.   Yet, do not grieve ;
>   She cannot fade ; though thou hast not thy bliss,
>   For ever wilt thou love, and she be fair."

And thus, in considering the process of Æsthetic
Empathy, we find ourselves suddenly back at our
original formula :   Beautiful means satisfactory
in contemplation, and contemplation not of Things
but of Shapes which are only Aspects of them.

CHAPTER XI

THE CHARACTER OF SHAPES

In my example of the Rising Mountain, I have been speaking as if Empathy invested the shapes we look at with only one mode of activity at a time. This, which I have assumed for the simplicity of exposition, is undoubtedly true in the case either of extremely simple shapes requiring *few* and homogeneous perceptive activities. It is true also in the case of shapes of which familiarity (as explained on p. 76) has made the actual perception very summary; for instance when, walking quickly among trees, we notice only what I may call their dominant empathic gesture of *thrusting* or *drooping* their branches, because habit allows us to pick out the most characteristic outlines. But, except in these and similar cases, the *movement* with which Empathy invests shapes is a great deal more complex, indeed we should speak more correctly of movements than of movement of lines. Thus the mountain rises, and does nothing but rise so long as we are taking stock only of the relation of its top with the plain, referring its lines solely to real or imaginary horizontals. But if, instead of our glance making a single swish upwards, we look at the two sides of the mountain successively and compare each with the other as well as with the plain, our impression (and our verbal description) will be that *one slope goes up while the other goes down*.   When the empathic scheme of the mountain thus ceases to be mere *rising* and becomes *rising plus descending*, the two *movements* with which we have thus invested that shape will be felt as being interdependent ; one side *goes down* because the other has *gone up*, or the movement rises *in order to* descend.   And if we look at a mountain chain we get a still more complex and co-ordinated empathic scheme, the peaks and valleys (as in my description of what the Man saw from his Hillside) appearing to us as a sequence of risings and sinkings with correlated intensities ; a slope *springing up* in proportion as the previously seen one *rushed down* ; the movements of the eye, slight and sketchy in themselves, awakening the composite dynamic memory of all our experience of the impetus gained by switch-back descent. Moreover this sequence, being a sequence, will awaken expectation of repetition, hence sense of rythm ; the long chain of peaks will seem to perform a dance, they will furl and unfurl like waves.   Thus as soon as we get a combination of empathic *forces* (for that is how they affect us) these will henceforth be in definite relation to one another.   But the relation need not be that of mere give and take and rythmical cooperation. Lines meeting one another may conflict, check, deflect one another ; or again resist each other's effort as the steady determination of a circumference resists, opposes a " Quos ego ! " to the rushing impact of the spokes of a wheel-pattern. And, along with the empathic suggestion of the mechanical forces experienced in ourselves, will come the empathic suggestion of spiritual characteristics : the lines will have aims, intentions, desires, moods ; their various little dramas of endeavour, victory, defeat or peacemaking, will, according to their dominant empathic suggestion, be lighthearted or languid, serious or futile, gentle or brutal ; inexorable, forgiving, hopeful, despairing, plaintive or proud, vulgar or dignified ; in fact patterns of visible lines will possess all the chief dynamic modes which determine the expressive-ness of music. But on the other hand there will remain innumerable emphatic combinations whose poignant significance escapes verbal classification because, as must be clearly understood, Empathy deals not directly with mood and emotion, but with dynamic conditions which enter into moods and emotions and take their names from them. Be this as it may, and definable or not in terms of human feeling, these various and variously combined (into coordinate scenes and acts) dramas enacted

by lines and curves and angles, take place not in
the marble or pigment embodying those contemplated shapes, but solely in ourselves, in what we
call our memory, imagination and feeling. Ours
are the energy, the effort, the victory or the peace
and cooperation ; and all the manifold modes of
swiftness or gravity, arduousness or ease, with which
their every minutest dynamic detail is fraught.
And since we are their only real actors, these empathic dramas of lines are bound to affect us, either
as corroborating or as thwarting our vital needs
and habits ; either as making our felt life easier or
more difficult, that is to say as bringing us peace
and joy, or depression and exasperation.

Quite apart therefore from the convenience or
not of the adjustments requisite for their ocular
measurement, and apart even from the facility or
difficulty of comparing and coordinating these
measurements, certain shapes and elements of shape
are made welcome to us, and other ones made un-
welcome, by the sole working of Empathy, which
identifies the modes of being and moving of lines
with our own. For this reason meetings of lines
which affect us as neither victory nor honourable
submission nor willing cooperation are felt to be
ineffectual and foolish. Lines also (like those of
insufficiently tapered Doric columns) which do
not *rise with enough impetus* because they do not

F

seem *to start with sufficient pressure at the base;*
oblique lines (as in certain imitation Gothic) which
lose their balance for lack of a countervailing *thrust*
against them, all these, and alas many hundreds
of other possible combinations, are detestable to
our feelings. And similarly we are fussed and
bored by the tentative lines, the uncoordinated
directions and impacts, of inferior, even if technically
expert and realistically learned draughtsmen, of
artists whose work may charm at first glance by
some vivid likeness or poetic suggestion, but reveal
with every additional day their complete insignificance as movement, their utter empathic nullity.
Indeed, if we analyse the censure ostensibly based
upon engineering considerations of material in-
stability, or on wrong perspective or anatomical
"out of drawing," we shall find that much of this
hostile criticism is really that of empathic un-
satisfactoriness, which escapes verbal detection
but is revealed by the finger *following*, as we say
(and that is itself an instance of empathy) the
movement, the development of, boring or fussing
lines.

Empathy explains not only the universally existing preferences with regard to shape, but also those
particular degrees of liking which are matters of
personal temperament and even of momentary
mood (*cf.* p. 131). Thus Mantegna, with his pre-

ponderance of horizontals and verticals will appeal
to one beholder as grave and reassuring, but repel
another beholder (or the same in a different mood)
as dull and lifeless ; while the unstable equilibrium
and syncopated rythm of Botticelli may either
fascinate or repel as morbidly excited. And
Leonardo's systems of whirling interlaced circles
will merely baffle (the "enigmatic" quality we
hear so much of) the perfunctory beholder, while
rewarding more adequate empathic imagination
by allowing us to live, for a while, in the modes of
the intensest and most purposeful and most
harmonious energy.

Intensity and purposefulness and harmony.
These are what everyday life affords but rarely to
our longings. And this is what, thanks to this
strange process of Empathy, a few inches of painted
canvas, will sometimes allow us to realise completely
and uninterruptedly. And it is no poetical metaphor
or metaphysical figment, but mere psychological
fact, to say that if the interlacing circles and pen-
tacles of a Byzantine floor-pattern absorb us in
satisfied contemplation, this is because the modes
of being which we are obliged to invest them with
are such as we vainly seek, or experience only to
lose, in our scattered or hustled existence.

CHAPTER XII

FROM THE SHAPE TO THE THING

SUCH are the satisfactions and dissatisfactions, impersonal and unpractical, we can receive, or in reality, give ourselves, in the contemplation of shape.

But life has little leisure for contemplation ; it demands *recognition*, inference and readiness for active adaptation. Or rather life forces us to deal with shapes mainly inasmuch as they indicate the actual or possible existence of other groups of qualities which may help or hurt us. Life hurries us into recognising *Things*.

Now the first peculiarity distinguishing *things* from *shapes* is *that they can occupy more or less cubic space :* we can hit up against them, displace them or be displaced by them, and in such process of displacing or resisting displacement, we become aware of two other peculiarities distinguishing things from shapes : they have *weight* in varying degrees and *texture* of various sorts. Otherwise expressed, things have *body*, they exist in three dimensional space ; while *shapes* although they are often aspects of things (say statues or vases) having body and cubic existence, shapes *as* shapes are two dimensional and bodiless.

So many of the critical applications of æsthetic, as well as of the historical problems of art-evolution are connected with this fact or rather the continued misunderstanding of it, that it is well to remind the Reader of what general Psychology can teach us of the perception of the Third Dimension. A very slight knowledge of cubic existence, in the sense of *relief*, is undoubtedly furnished as the stereoscope furnishes it, by the inevitable slight divergence between the two eyes ; an even more infinitesimal dose of such knowledge is claimed for the surfaces of each eye separately. But whatever notions of three-dimensional space might have been developed from such rudiments, the perception of cubic existence which we actually possess and employ, is undeniably based upon the incomparably more important data afforded by locomotion, under which term I include even the tiny pressure of a finger against a surface, and the exploration of a hollow tooth by the tip of the tongue. The muscular adjustments made in such locomotion become associated by repetition with the two-dimensional arrangements of colour and light revealed by the eye, the two-dimensional being thus turned into the three-dimensional in our everyday experience. But the mistakes we occasionally make, for instance taking a road seen from above for a church-tower projecting out of the plain, or the perspective of a mountain range for its cubic shape, occasionally reveal that we do not really *see* three-dimensional objects, but merely *infer* them by connecting visual data with the result of locomotor experience. The truth of this commonplace of psychology can be tested by the experiment of making now one, now the other, colour of a floor pattern seem convex or concave according as we think of it as a light flower on a dark ground, or as a white cavity banked in by a dark ridge. And when the philistine (who may be you or me!) exclaims against the "out of drawing" and false perspective of unfamiliar styles of painting, he is, nine times out of ten, merely expressing his inability to identify two-dimensional shapes as "representing" three-dimensional things; so far proving that we do not decipher the cubic relations of a picture until we have guessed what that picture is supposed to stand for. And this is my reason for saying that visible shapes, though they may be aspects of cubic objects, have no body; and that the thought of their volume, their weight and their texture, is due to an interruption of our contemplation of shape by an excursion among the recollections of qualities which shapes, *as* shapes, cannot possess.

And here I would forestall the Reader's objection

that the feeling of effort and resistance, essential
to all our empathic dealings with two-dimensional
shapes, must, after all, be due to *weight*, which we
have just described as a quality shapes cannot
possess. My answer is that Empathy has extracted
and schematised effort and resistance by the elimination of the thought of weight, as by the elimination
of the awareness of our bodily tensions ; and that
it is just this elimination of all incompatible qualities
which allows us to attribute activities to these two-
dimensional shapes, and to feel these activities, with
a vividness undiminished by the thought of any
other circumstances.

With cubic existence (and its correlative three-
dimensional space), with weight and texture we
have therefore got from the contemplated shape
to a thought alien to that shape and its contemplation. The thought, to which life and its needs and
dangers has given precedence over every other :
What *Thing* is behind this shape, what qualities
must be inferred from this *aspect* ? After the
possibility of occupying so much space, the most
important quality which things can have for our
hopes and fears, is *the possibility of altering their
occupation of space ;* not our locomotion, but *theirs.*
I call it *locomotion* rather than *movement*, because
we have *direct* experience only of our own movements, and *infer* similar movement in other beings

and objects because of their change of place either across our motionless eye or across some other object whose relation to our motionless eye remains unchanged. I call it *locomotion* also to accentuate its difference from the *movement* attributed to the shape of the Rising Mountain, movement *felt* by us to be going on but not expected to result in any change of the mountain's space relations, which are precisely what would be altered by the mountain's *locomotion*.

The *practical* question about a shape is therefore : Does it warrant the inference of a *thing* able to change its position in three-dimensional space ? to advance or recede from us ? And if so in what manner ? Will it, like a loose stone, fall upon us ? like flame, rise towards us ? like water, spread over us ? Or will it change its place only if *we* supply the necessary *locomotion* ? Briefly : is the thing of which we see the shape inert or active ? And if this shape belongs to a thing possessing activity of its own, is its locomotion of that slow regular kind we call the growth and spreading of plants ? Or of the sudden, wilful kind we know in animals and men ? What does this shape tell us of such more formidable locomotion ? Are these details of curve and colour to be interpreted into jointed limbs, can the *thing* fling out laterally, run after us, can it catch and swallow us ? Or is it such that *we* can do thus by it ? Does this shape suggest the thing's possession of desires and purposes which we can deal with ? And if so, *why is it where it is ?* Whence does it come ? What is it going to do ? What is it *thinking* of (if it can think) ? How will it *feel* towards us (if it can feel) ? What would it say (if it could speak) ? What will be its future and what may have been its past ? To sum all up : What does the presence of this shape lead us to think and do and feel ?

Such are a few of the thoughts started by that shape and the possibility of its belonging to a thing. And even when, as we shall sometimes find, they continually return back to the shape and play round and round it in centrifugal and centripetal alternations, yet all these thoughts are excursions, however brief, from the world of definite unchanging shapes into that of various and ever varying things ; interruptions, even if (as we shall later see) intensifying interruptions, of that concentrated and co-ordinated contemplation of shapes, with which we have hitherto dealt. And these excursions, and a great many more, from the world of shapes into that of things, are what we shall deal with, when we come to Art, under the heading of *representation* and *suggestion,* or, as is usually said, of *subject* and *expression* as opposed to *form.*

CHAPTER XIII

FROM THE THING TO THE SHAPE

THE necessities of analysis and exposition have led us from the Shape to the Thing, from æsthetic contemplation to discursive and practical thinking. But, as the foregoing chapter itself suggests, the real order of precedence, both for the individual and the race, is inevitably the reverse, since without a primary and dominant interest in things no creatures would have survived to develop an interest in shapes.

Indeed, considering the imperative need for an ever abbreviated and often automatic system of human reactions to sense data, it is by no means easy to understand (and the problem has therefore been utterly neglected) how mankind ever came to evolve any process as lengthy and complicated as that form-contemplation upon which all æsthetic preference depends. I will hazard the suggestion that familiarity with shapes took its original evolutional utility, as well as its origin, from the dangers of over rapid and uncritical inference concerning the qualities of things and man's proper reactions towards them. It was necessary, no doubt, that

the roughest suggestion of a bear's growl and a
bear's outline should send our earliest ancestors
into their sheltering caves. But the occasional
discovery that the bear was not a bear but some
more harmless and edible animal must have brought
about a comparison, a discrimination between the
visible aspects of the two beasts, and a mental
storage of their difference in shape, gait and colour.
Similarly the deluding resemblance between
poisonous and nutritious fruits and roots, would
result, as the resemblance between the nurse's
finger and nipple results with the infant, in attention
to visible details, until the acquisition of vivid
mental images became the chief item of the savage
man's education, as it still is of the self-education
of the modern child. This evolution of interest in
visible aspects would of course increase tenfold as
soon as mankind took to making things whose
usefulness (*i.e.* their still non-existent qualities)
might be jeopardised by a mistake concerning their
shape. For long after *over* and *under*, *straight* and
oblique, *right* and *left*, had become habitual perceptions in dealing with food and fuel, the effective
aim of a stone, the satisfactory ˙flight of an arrow,
would be discovered to depend upon more or less of
what we call horizontals and perpendiculars, curves
and angles ; and the stability of a fibrous tissue
upon the intervals of crossing and recrossing, the

rythmical or symmetrical arrangements revealed
by the hand or eye. In short, *making*, being inevitably *shaping*, would have developed a more
and more accurate perception and recollection of
every detail of shape. And not only would there
arise a comparison between one shape and another
shape, but between the shape actually under one's
eyes and the shape no longer present, between the
shape as it really was and the shape as it ought to
be. Thus in the very course of practical making
of things there would come to be little interludes,
recognised as useful, first of more and more careful
looking and comparing, and then of real contemplation : contemplation of the arrow-head you were
chipping, of the mat you were weaving, of the pot
you were rubbing into shape ; contemplation also
of the *other* arrow-head or mat or pot existing only
in your wishes ; of the shape you were trying to
obtain with a premonitory emotion of the effect
which its peculiarities would produce when once
made visible to your eye ! For the man cutting
the arrow-head, the woman plaiting the mat, becoming familiar with the appropriate shapes of each
and thinking of the various individual arrow-heads
or mats of the same type, *would become aware of
the different effect which such shapes had on the person
who looked at them*. Some of these shapes would
be so dull, increasing the tediousness of chipping

and filing or of laying strand over strand ; others
so alert, entertaining and likeable, as if they were
helping in the work ; others, although equally
compatible with utility, fussing or distressing one,
never doing what one expected their lines and curves
to do. To these suppositions I would add a few
more suggestions regarding the evolution of shape-
contemplation out of man's perfunctory and
semi-automatic seeing of " Things." The handicraftsman, armourer, weaver, or potter, benefits by
his own and his forerunners' practical experience
of which shape is the more adapted for use and
wear, and which way to set about producing it ;
his technical skill becomes half automatic, so that
his eye and mind, acting as mere overseers to his
muscles, have plenty of time for contemplation so
long as everything goes right and no new moves
have to be made. And once the handicraftsman
contemplates the shape as it issues from his fingers,
his mind will be gripped by that liking or disliking
expressed by the words " beautiful " and " ugly."
Neither is this all. The owner of a weapon or a
vessel or piece of tissue, is not always intent upon
employing it ; in proportion to its usefulness and
durability and to the amount of time, good luck,
skill or strength required to make or to obtain it,
this chattel will turn from a slave into a comrade.
It is furbished or mended, displayed to others,

boasted over, perhaps sung over as Alan Breck sang over his sword. The owner's eye (and not less that of the man envious of the owner !) caresses its shape ; and its shape, all its well-known ins-and-outs and ups-and-downs, haunts the memory, ready to start into vividness whenever similar objects come under comparison. Now what holds good of primæval and savage man holds good also of civilized, perhaps even of ourselves among our machine made and easily replaced properties. The shape of the things we make and use offers itself for contemplation in those interludes of inattention which are half of the rythm of all healthful work. And it is this normal rythm of attention swinging from effort to ease, which explains how art has come to be a part of life, how mere aspects have acquired for our feelings an importance rivalling that of things.

I therefore commend to the Reader the now somewhat unfashionable hypothesis of Semper and his school, according to which the first preference for beauty of shape must be sought for in those arts like stone and metal work, pottery and weaving, which give opportunities for repetition, reduplica-tion, hence rythm and symmetry, and whose material and technique produce what are called geometric patterns, meaning such as exist in two dimensions and do not imitate the shapes of real objects. This theory has been discredited by the discovery that very primitive and savage mankind possessed a kind of art of totally different nature, and which analogy with that of children suggests as earlier than that of pattern : the art which the ingenious hypothesis of Mr Henry Balfour derives from recognition of accidental resemblances between the shapes and stains of wood or stone and such creatures and objects as happen to be uppermost in the mind of the observer, who cuts or paints whatever may be needed to complete the likeness and enable others to perceive the suggestion. Whether or not this was its origin, there seems to have existed in earliest times such an art of a strictly representative kind, serving (like the spontaneous art of children) to evoke the idea of whatever was interesting to the craftsman and his clients, and doubtless practically to have some desirable magic effect upon the realities of things. But (to return to the hypothesis of the æsthetic primacy of geometric and non-representative art) it is certain that although such early representations occasionally attain marvellous life-likeness and anatomical correctness, yet they do not at first show any corresponding care for symmetrical and rythmical arrangement. The bisons and wild boars, for instance, of the Altamira cave frescoes, do indeed display vigour and beauty in the lines constituting them, proving that successful dealing with shape, even if appealing only to practical interest, inevitably calls forth the empathic imagination of the more gifted artists; but these marvellously drawn figures are all huddled together or scattered as out of a rag-bag; and, what is still more significant, they lack that insistence on the feet which not only suggests ground beneath them but, in so doing, furnishes a horizontal by which to start, measure and take the bearings of all other lines. These astonishing palæolithic artists (and indeed the very earliest Egyptian and Greek ones) seem to have thought only of the living models and their present and future movements, and to have cared as little for lines and angles as the modern children whose drawings have been instructively compared with theirs by Levinstein and others. I therefore venture to suggest that such æsthetically essential attention to direction and composition must have been applied to representative art when its realistic figures were gradually incorporated into the patterns of the weaver and the potter. Such "stylisation" is still described by art historians as a "degeneration" due to unintelligent repetition; but it was on the contrary the integrating process by which the representative element was subjected to such æsthetic preferences as had been established in the manufacture of objects whose usefulness or whose production involved accurate measurement and equilibrium as in the case of pottery or weapons, or rythmical reduplication as in that of textiles.

Be this question as it may (and the increasing study of the origin and evolution of human faculties will some day settle it !) we already know enough to affirm that while in the very earliest art the shape-element and the element of representation are usually separate, the two get gradually combined as civilisation advances, and the shapes originally interesting only inasmuch as suggestions (hence as magical equivalents) of things, and employed for religious, recording, or self-expressive purposes, become subjected to selection and re-arrangement by the habit of avoiding disagreeable perceptive and empathic activities and the desire of giving scope to agreeable ones. Nay the whole subsequent history of painting and sculpture could be formulated as the perpetual starting up of new representative interests, new interests in *things*, their spatial existence, locomotion, anatomy, their reaction to light, and also their psychological and dramatic possibilities ; and the subordination of these ever-changing interests in things to the unchanging habit of arranging visible shapes so as to diminish opportunities for the contemplative dissatisfaction and increase opportunities for the contemplative satisfaction to which we attach the respective names of " ugly " and " beautiful."

G

CHAPTER XIV

THE AIMS OF ART

WE have thus at last got to Art, which the Reader
may have expected to be dealt with at the outset
of a primer on the Beautiful.

Why this could not be the case, will be more and
more apparent in my remaining chapters. And,
in order to make those coming chapters easier to
grasp, I may as well forestall and tabulate the
views they embody upon the relation between the
Beautiful and Art. These generalisations are as
follows :

Although it is historically probable that the habit
of avoiding ugliness and seeking beauty of shape
may have been originally established by utilitarian
attention to the non-imitative (" geometrical ")
shapes of weaving, pottery and implement-making,
and transferred from these crafts to the shapes
intended to represent or imitate natural objects,
yet the distinction between *Beautiful* and *Ugly*
does not belong either solely or necessarily to what
we call *Art*. Therefore the satisfaction of the shape-
perceptive or æsthetic preferences must not be
confused with any of the many and various other

aims and activities to which art is due and by
which it is carried on. Conversely : although in its
more developed phases, and after the attainment
of technical facility, art has been differentiated
from other human employment by its foreseeing
the possibility of shape-contemplation and therefore
submitting itself to what I have elsewhere called
the *æsthetic imperative*, yet art has invariably started
from some desire other than that of affording
satisfactory shape-contemplation, with the one exception of cases where it has been used to keep or
reproduce opportunities of such shape contemplation already accidentally afforded by natural shapes,
say, those of flowers or animals or landscapes,
or even occasionally of human beings, which had
already been enjoyed as beautiful. All art therefore, except that of children, savages, ignoramuses
and extreme innovators, invariably avoids ugly
shapes and seeks for beautiful ones ; *but art does
this while pursuing all manner of different aims.*
These non-æsthetic aims of art may be roughly
divided into (A) the making of useful objects ranging
from clothes to weapons and from a pitcher to a
temple ; (B) the registering or transmitting of facts
and their visualising, as in portraits, historical
pictures or literature, and book illustration ; and
(C) the awakening, intensifying or maintaining of
definite emotional states, as especially by music

and literature, but also by painting and architecture when employed as " aids to devotion." And these large classes may again be subdivided and connected, if the Reader has a mind to, into utilitarian, social, ritual, sentimental, scientific and other aims, some of them not countenanced or not avowed by contemporary morality.

How the æsthetic imperative, i.e. the necessities of satisfactory shape-contemplation, qualifies and deflects the pursuit of such non-æsthetic aims of art can be shown by comparing, for instance, the mere audible devices for conveying conventional meaning and producing and keeping up emotional conditions, viz. the hootings and screechings of modern industrialism no less than the ritual noises of savages, with the arrangements of well constituted pitch, rythm, tonality and harmony in which military, religious or dance music has disguised its non-æsthetic functions of conveying signals or acting on the nerves. Whatever is unnecessary for either of these motives (or any others) for making a noise, can be put to the account of the desire to avoid ugliness and enjoy beauty. But the workings of the æsthetic imperative can best be studied in the Art of the visual-representative group, and especially in painting, which allows us to follow the interplay of the desire to be told (or tell) *facts about things* with the desire to *contemplate shapes*, and to contemplate them (otherwise we should *not* contemplate !) with sensuous, intellectual and empathic satisfaction.

This brings us back to the Third Dimension, of which the possession is, as have we seen, the chief difference between *Things*, which can alter their aspect in the course of their own and our actions, and *Shapes*, which can only be contemplated by our bodily and mental eye, and neither altered nor thought of as altered without more or less jeopardising their identity.

I daresay the Reader may not have been satisfied with the reference to the locomotor nature of cubic perception as sufficient justification of my thus connecting cubic existence with Things rather than with Shapes, and my implying that æsthetic preference, due to the sensory, intellectual and empathic factors of perception, is applicable only to the two other dimensions. And the Reader's incredulity and surprise will have been all the greater, because recent art-criticism has sedulously inculcated that the suggestion of cubic existence is the chief function of pictorial genius, and the realisation of such cubic existence the highest delight which pictures can afford to their worthy beholder. This particular notion, entirely opposed to the facts of visual perception and visual empathy, will repay discussion, inasmuch as it accidentally affords an easy

entrance into a subject which has hitherto presented
inextricable confusion, namely the relations of
Form and *Subject*, or, as I have accustomed the
Reader to consider them, the *contemplated Shape*
and the *thought-of Thing*.

Let us therefore examine why art-criticism
should lay so great a stress on the suggestion and
the acceptance of that suggestion, of three-dimensional existence in paintings. *In paintings.* For
this alleged æsthetic desideratum ceases to be a
criterion of merit when we come to sculpture, about
which critics are more and more persistently teaching
(and with a degree of reason) that one of the greatest
merits of the artist, and of the greatest desiderata
of the beholder, is precisely the reduction of real
cubic existence by avoiding all projection beyond
a unified level, that is to say by making a solid
block of stone look as if it were a representation
on a flat surface. This contradiction explains
the origin of the theory giving supreme pictorial
importance to the Third Dimension. For art
criticism though at length (thanks especially to
the sculptor Hildebrand) busying itself also with
plastic art, has grown up mainly in connexion
with painting. Now in painting the greatest
scientific problem, and technical difficulty, has
been the suggestion of three-dimensional existences
by pigments applied to a two-dimensional surface ;

and this problem has naturally been most successfully handled by the artists possessing most energy and imagination, and equally naturally shirked or bungled or treated parrot-wise by the artists of less energy and imagination. And, as energy and imagination also show themselves in finer perception, more vivid empathy and more complex dealings with shapes which are only two-dimensional, it has come about that the efficient and original solutions of the cubic problem have coincided, *ceteris paribus*, with the production of pictures whose two-dimensional qualities have called forth the adjective *beautiful*, and *beautiful* in the most intense and complicated manner. Hence successful treatment of cubic suggestion has become an habitual (and threatens to become a rule-of-thumb) criterion of pictorial merit ; the more so that qualities of two-dimensional shape, being intrinsic and specific, are difficult to run to ground and describe ; whereas the quality of three-dimensional suggestion is ascertainable by mere comparison between the shapes in the picture and the shapes afforded by real things when seen in the same perspective and lighting. Most people can judge whether an apple in a picture " looks as if " it were solid, round, heavy and likely to roll off a sideboard in the same picture ; and some people may even, when the picture has no other claims on their interest,

experience incipient muscular contractions such as
would eventually interfere with a real apple rolling off a real sideboard. Apples and sideboards
offer themselves to the meanest experience and can
be dealt with adequately in everyday language,
whereas the precise curves and angles, the precise
relations of directions and impacts, of parts to
whole, which together make up the identity of a
two-dimensional shape, are indeed perceived and
felt by the attentive beholder, but not habitually
analysed or set forth in words. Moreover the
creation of two-dimensional shapes satisfying to
contemplation depends upon two very different
factors : on traditional experience with regard to
the more general arrangements of lines, and on
individual energy and sensitiveness, i.e. on genius
in carrying out, and ringing changes on, such traditional arrangements. And the possession of tradition or genius, although no doubt the most important
advantage of an artist, happens not to be one to
which he can apply himself as to a problem. On
the other hand a problem to be solved is eternally
being pressed upon every artist ; pressed on him
by his clients, by the fashion of his time and also
by his own self inasmuch as he is a man interested
not only in *shapes* but in *things*. And thus we are
back at the fact that the problem given to the
painter to solve by means of lines and colours on a

flat surface, is the problem of telling us something new or something important about *things* : what things are made of, how they will react to our doings, how they move, what they feel and think ; and above all, I repeat it, what amount of space they occupy with reference to the space similarly occupied, in present or future, by other things including ourselves.

Our enquiry into the excessive importance attributed by critics to pictorial suggestion of cubic existence has thus led us back to the conclusion contained in previous chapters, namely that beauty depending negatively on ease of visual perception, and positively upon emphatic corroboration of our dynamic habits, is a quality of *aspects*, independent of cubic existence and every other possible quality of *things* ; except in so far as the thought of three-dimensional, and other, qualities of things may interfere with the freedom and readiness of mind requisite for such highly active and sensitive processes as those of empathic form interpretation. But the following chapter will, I trust, make it clear that such interference of the *Thought about Things* with the *Contemplation of Shapes* is essential to the rythm of our mental life, and therefore a chief factor in all artistic production and appreciation.

CHAPTER XV

ATTENTION TO SHAPES

To explain how art in general, and any art in particular, succeeds in reconciling these contradictory demands, I must remind the Reader of what I said (p. 93) about the satisfactory or unsatisfactory possibilities of shapes having begun to be noticed in the moments of slackened attention to the processes of manufacturing the objects embodying those shapes, and in the intervals between practical employment of these more or less *shapely* objects. And I must ask him to connect with these remarks a previous passage (p. 44) concerning the intermittent nature of normal acts of attention, and their alternation as constituting *on-and-off beats*. The deduction from these two converging statements is that, contrary to the a-priori theories making aesthetic contemplation an exception, a kind of bank holiday, to daily life, it is in reality one-half of daily life's natural and healthy rythm. That the real state of affairs, as revealed by psychological experiment and observation, should have escaped the notice of so many æstheticians, is probably due to their theories starting from artistic production rather than from æsthetic appreciation, without which art would after all probably never have come into existence.

The production of the simplest work of art cannot indeed be thought of as one of the alternations of everyday attention, because it is a long, complex and repeatedly resumed process, a whole piece of life, including in itself hundreds and thousands of alternations of *doing* and *looking*, of discursive thinking of aims and ways and means and of contemplation of æsthetic results. For even the humblest artist has to think of whatever objects or processes his work aims at representing, conveying or facilitating; and to think also of the objects, marble, wood, paints, voices, and of the processes, drawing, cutting, harmonic combining, by which he attempts to compass one of the abovementioned results. The artist is not only an æsthetically appreciative person; he is, in his own way, a man of science and a man of practical devices, an expert, a craftsman and an engineer. To produce a work of art is not an interlude in his life, but his life's main business; and he therefore stands apart, as every busy specialist must, from the business of other specialists, of those ministering to mankind's scientific and practical interests.

But while it takes days, months, sometimes years

to produce a work of art, it may require (the process has been submitted to exact measurement by the stop-watch) not minutes but seconds, to take stock of that work of art in such manner as to carry away its every detail of shape, and to continue dealing with it in memory. The unsuspected part played by memory explains why æsthetic contemplation can be and normally is, an intermittent function alternating with practical doing and thinking. It is in memory, though memory dealing with what we call the present, that we gather up parts into wholes and turn consecutive measurements into simultaneous relations ; and it is probably in memory that we deal empathically with shapes, investing their already perceived directions and relations with the remembered qualities of our own activities, aims and moods. And similarly it is thanks to memory that the brief and intermittent acts of æsthetic appreciation are combined into a network of contemplation which intermeshes with our other thoughts and doings, and yet remains different from them, as the restorative functions of life remain different from life's expenditure, although interwoven with them. Every Reader with any habit of self-observation knows how poignant an impression of beauty may be got, as through the window of an express train, in the intermittence of practical business or abstract thinking, nay even

in what I have called the *off-beat* of deepest personal
emotion, the very stress of the practical, intellectual
or personal instant (for the great happenings of life
are measured in seconds !) apparently driving in
by contrast, or conveying on its excitement, that
irrelevant æsthetic contents of the *off-beat* of
attention. And while the practical or intellectual
interest changes, while the personal emotion sub-
sides, that æsthetic impression remains ; remains
or recurs, united, through every intermittence, by
the feeling of identity, that identity which, like
the rising of the mountain, is due to the reiterative
nature of shape-contemplation : the fragments of
melody may be interrupted in our memory by all
manner of other thoughts, but they will recur and
coalesce, and recurring and coalescing, bring with
them the particular mood which their rythms and
intervals have awakened in us and awaken once
more.

That diagrammatic Man on the Hill in reality
thought away from the landscape quite as much as
his practical and scientific companions ; what he
did, and they did not, was to think *back* to it ; and
think back to it always with the same references
of lines and angles, the same relations of directions
and impacts, of parts and wholes. And perhaps
the restorative, the healing quality of æsthetic
contemplation is due, in large part, to the fact that,

in the perpetual flux of action and thought, it represents reiteration and therefore stability.

Be that as it may, the intermittent but recurrent character of shape contemplation, the fact that it is inconceivably brief and amazingly repetitive, that it has the essential quality of identity because of reiteration, all this explains also two chief points of our subject. First : how an æsthetic impression, intentionally or accidentally conveyed in the course of wholly different interests, can become a constant accompaniment to the shifting preoccupations of existence, like the remembered songs which sing themselves silently in our mind and the remembered landscapes becoming an intangible background to our ever-varying thoughts. And, secondly, it explains how art can fulfil the behests of our changing and discursive interest in things while satisfying the imperious unchanging demands of the contemplated preference for beautiful aspects. And thus we return to my starting-point in dealing with art : that art is conditioned by the desire for beauty while pursuing entirely different aims, and executing any one of a variety of wholly independent non-æsthetic tasks.

CHAPTER XVI

INFORMATION ABOUT THINGS

AMONG the facts which Painting is set to tell us
about things, the most important, after cubic existence, is Locomotion.   Indeed in the development of
the race as well as in that of the individual, pictorial
attention to locomotion seems to precede attention
to cubic existence.   For when the palæolithic, or
the Egyptian draughtsman, or even the Sixth
Century Greek, unites profile legs and head with a
full-face chest ; and when the modern child sup-
plements the insufficiently projecting full-face nose
by a profile nose tacked on where we expect the
ear, we are apt to think that these mistakes are
due to indifference to the cubic nature of things.
The reverse is, however, the case.   The primitive
draughtsman and the child are recording impressions received in the course of the locomotion either
of the thing looked at or of the spectator.   When
they unite whatever consecutive aspects are most
significant and at the same time easiest to copy,
they are in the clutches of their cubic experience,
and what they are indifferent about, perhaps un-
conscious of, is the *two-dimensional* appearance

which a body presents when its parts are seen simultaneously and therefore from a single point of view. The progress of painting is always from representing the Consecutive to representing the Simultaneous; perspective, foreshortening, and later, light and shade, being the scientific and technical means towards this end.

Upon our knowledge of the precise stage of such pictorial development depends our correct recognition of what things, and particularly what spatial relations and locomotion, of things, the painter is intended to represent. Thus when a Byzantine draughtsman puts his figures in what look to us as superposed tiers, he is merely trying to convey their existence behind one another on a common level. And what we take for the elaborate contortions of athletes and Athenas on Sixth Century vases turns out to be nothing but an archaic representation of ordinary walking and running.

The suggestion of locomotion depends furthermore on anatomy. What the figures of a painting are intended to be doing, what they are intended to have just done and to be going to do, in fact all questions about their action and business, are answered by reference to their bodily structure and its real or supposed possibilities. The same applies to expression of mood.

The impassiveness of archaic Apollos is more likely

to be due to anatomical difficulties in displacing arms and legs, than to lack of emotion on the part of artists who were, after all, contemporaries either of Sappho or Pindar. And it is more probable that the sculptors of Ægina were still embarrassed about the modelling of lips and cheeks than that, having Homer by heart, they imagined his heroes to die silently and with a smirk.

I have entered into this question of perspective and anatomy, and given the above examples, because they will bring home to the reader one of the chief principles deduced from our previous examination into the psychology of our subject, namely that *all thinking about things is thinking away from the Shapes suggesting those things, since it involves knowledge which the Shapes in themselves do not afford.* And I have insisted particularly upon the dependence of representations of locomotion upon knowledge of three-dimensional existence, because, before proceeding to the relations of Subject and Form in painting, I want to impress once more upon the reader the distinction between the *locomotion of things* (locomotion active or passive) and what, in my example of the *mountain which rises*, I have called the *empathic movement of lines.* Such *movement of lines* we have seen to be a scheme of activity suggested by our own activity in taking stock of a two-dimensional-shape ; an *idea,* or *feeling* of activity

H

which we, being normally unaware of its origin in
ourselves, project into the shape which has suggested
it, precisely as we project our sensation of *red* from
our own eye and mind into the object which has
deflected the rays of light in such a way as to give
us that *red* sensation.   Such *empathic*, attributed,
movements of lines are therefore intrinsic qualities
of the shapes whose active perception has called
them forth in our imagination and feeling ;   and
being qualities of the shapes, they inevitably change
with every alteration which a shape undergoes,
every shape, actively perceived, having its own
special *movement of lines* ;   and every *movement of
lines*, or *combination of movements of lines* existing
in proportion as we go over and over again the
particular shape of which it is a quality.   The
case is absolutely reversed when we perceive or
think of, the *locomotion of things*. The thought
of a thing's locomotion, whether locomotion done
by itself or inflicted by something else, necessi-
tates our thinking away from the particular shape
before us to another shape more or less different.
In other words locomotion necessarily alters what
we are looking at or thinking of. If we think of
Michel Angelo's seated Moses as getting up, we think
away from the approximately pyramidal shape of
the statue to the elongated oblong of a standing
figure.   If we think of the horse of Marcus Aurelius

as taking the next step, we think of a straightened leg set on the ground instead of a curved leg suspended in the air. And if we think of the Myronian Discobolus as letting go his quoit and " recovering," we think of the matchless spiral composition as unwinding and straightening itself into a shape as different as that of a tree is different from that of a shell.

The pictorial representation of locomotion affords therefore the extreme example of the difference between discursive thinking about things and contemplation of shape. Bearing this example in mind we cannot fail to understand that, just as the thought of *locomotion* is opposed to the thought of *movement of lines*, so, in more or less degree, the thought of the objects and actions represented by a picture or statue, is likely to divert the mind from the pictorial and plastic shapes which do the representing. And we can also understand that the problem unconsciously dealt with by all art (though by no means consciously by every artist) is to execute the order of suggesting interesting facts about things in a manner such as to satisfy at the same time the æsthetic demand for shapes which shall be satisfactory to contemplate. Unless this demand for sensorially, intellectually and empathically desirable shapes be complied with a work of art may be interesting as a diagram, a record or an illustration, but once the facts have been conveyed and assimilated with the rest of our knowledge, there will remain a shape which we shall never want to lay eyes upon. I cannot repeat too often that the differentiating characteristic of art is that it gives its works a value for contemplation independent of their value for fact-transmission, their value as nerve-and-emotion-excitant and of their value for immediate, for practical, utility. This æsthetic value, depending upon the unchanging processes of perception and empathy, asserts itself in answer to every act of contemplative attention, and is as enduring and intrinsic as the other values are apt to be momentary and relative. A Greek vase with its bottom knocked out and with a scarce intelligible incident of obsolete mythology portrayed upon it, has claims upon our feelings which the most useful modern mechanism ceases to have even in the intervals of its use, and which the newspaper, crammed full of the most important tidings, loses as soon as we have taken in its contents.

CHAPTER XVII

THE CO-OPERATION OF THINGS AND SHAPES

DURING the Middle Ages and up to recent times the chief task of painting has been, ostensibly, the telling and re-telling of the same Scripture stories ; and, incidentally, the telling them with the addition of constantly new items of information about *things* : their volume, position, structure, locomotion, light and shade and interactions of texture and atmosphere ; to which items must be added others of psychological or (pseudo)-historical kind, how it all came about, in what surroundings and dresses, and accompanied by what feelings. This task, official and unofficial, is in no way different from those fulfilled by the man of science and the practical man, both of whom are perpetually dealing with additional items of information. But mark the difference in the artist's way of accomplishing this task : a scientific fact is embodied in the progressive mass of knowledge, assimilated, corrected ; a practical fact is taken in consideration, built upon ; but the treatise, the newspaper or letter, once it has conveyed these facts, is forgotten or discarded. The work of art on the contrary is remembered and

117

cherished ; or at all events it is made with the
intention of being remembered and cherished. In
other words and as I shall never tire of repeating,
the differentiating characteristic of art is that it
makes *you think back to the shape* once that shape
has conveyed its message or done its business of
calling your attention or exciting your emotions.
And the first and foremost problem, for instance
of painting, is that of preventing the beholder's
eye from being carried, by lines of perspective,
outside the frame and even persistently out of the
centre of the picture ; the sculptor (and this is the
real reason of the sculptor Hildebrand's rules for
plastic composition) obeying a similar necessity of
keeping the beholder's eye upon the main masses
of his statue, instead of diverting it, by projections
at different distances, like the sticking out arms
and hands of Roman figures. So much for the eye
of the body : the beholder's curiosity must similarly not be carried outside the work of art by, for
instance, an incomplete figure (legs without a body !)
or an unfinished gesture, this being, it seems to me,
the only real reason against the representation of
extremely rapid action and transitory positions.
But when the task of conveying information implies
that the beholder's thoughts be deliberately led
from what is represented to what is not, then this
centrifugal action is dealt with so as to produce a

centripetal one back to the work of art : the painter suggests questions of *how* and *why* which get their answers in some item obliging you to take fresh stock of the picture. What is the meaning of the angels and evidently supernatural horseman in the foreground of Raphael's *Heliodorus?* Your mind flies to the praying High Priest in the central recess of the temple, and in going backwards and forwards between him, the main group and the scattered astonished bystanders, you are effectually enclosed within the arches of that marvellous composition, and induced to explore every detail of its lovely and noble constituent shapes.

The methods employed thus to keep the beholder's attention inside the work of art while suggesting things beyond it, naturally vary with the exact nature of the non-æsthetic task which has been set to the artist ; and with the artist's individual endowment and even more with the traditional artistic formulæ of his country and time : Raphael's devices in *Heliodorus* could not have been compassed by Giotto ; and, on the other hand, would have been rejected as " academic " by Manet. But whatever the methods employed, and however obviously they reveal that satisfactory form-contemplation is the one and invariable *condition* as distinguished from the innumerable varying *aims*, of all works of art, the Reader will find them discussed not as methods for securing attention to the shape, but as methods of employing that shape for some non-æsthetic purpose; whether that purpose be inducing you to drink out of a cup by making its shape convenient or suggestive; or inducing you to buy a particular commodity by branding its name and virtues on your mind; or fixing your thoughts on the Madonna's sorrows; or awaking your sympathy for Isolde's love tragedy. And yet it is evident that the artist who shaped the cup or designed the poster would be horribly disappointed if you thought only of drinking or of shopping and never gave another look to the cup or the poster; and that Perugino or Wagner would have died of despair if his suggestion of the Madonna's sorrows or of Isolde's love-agonies had been so efficacious as to prevent anybody from looking twice at the fresco or listening to the end of the opera. This inversion of the question is worth inquiring into, because, like the analogous paradox about the pictorial " realisation " of cubic existence, it affords an illustration of some of the psychological intricacies of the relation between Art and the Beautiful. This is how I propose to explain it.

The task to which an artist is set varies from one work to another, while the shapes employed for the purpose are, as already said, limited by his

powers and especially by the precise moment in
artistic evolution. The artist therefore thinks of
his available shapes as something given, as *means*,
and the subject he is ordered to represent (or the
emotion he is commissioned to elicit) as the all-
important *aim*. Thus he thinks of himself (and
makes the critic think of him) not as preventing
the represented subject or expressed emotion from
withdrawing the beholder from the artistic shapes,
but, on the contrary, as employing these artistic
shapes for the sole purpose of that representation
or emotional expression. And this most explicable
inversion of the real state of affairs ends by making
the beholder believe that what *he* cares for in a
masterpiece is not the beauty of shape which only
a masterpiece could have, but the efficacy of bringing
home a subject or expressing an emotion which
could be just as efficaciously represented or elicited
by the vilest daub or the wretchedest barrel organ !
   This inevitable, and I believe, salutary illusion
of the artist, is further increased by the fact that
while the artist's ingenuity must be bent on avoiding irrelevance and diminishing opportunities for
ugliness, the actual beauty of the shapes he is
creating arises from the depths of his unreasoned,
traditional and organised consciousness, from
activities which might be called automatic if they
were not accompanied by a critical feeling that

what is produced thus spontaneously and inevitably is either turning out as it must and should, or, contrariwise, insists upon turning out exactly as it *should not*. The particular system of curves and angles, of directions and impacts of lines, the particular " whole-and-part " scheme of, let us say, Michelangelo, is due to his modes of æsthetic perceiving, feeling, living, added to those of all the other artists whose peculiarities have been averaged in what we call the school whence Michelangelo issued. He can no more depart from these shapes than he can paint Rembrandt's Pilgrims of Emmaus without Rembrandt's science of light and shade and Rembrandt's oil-and-canvas technique. There is no alternative, hence no choice, hence no feeling of a problem to resolve, in this question of shapes to employ. But there are dozens of alternatives and of acts of choice, there is a whole series of problems when Michelangelo sets to employing these inevitable shapes to telling the Parting of the Light from the Darkness, or the Creation of Adam on the Vault of the Sixtine, and to surrounding the stories from Genesis with Prophets and Sibyls and Ancestors of Christ. Is the ceiling to remain a unity, or be broken up into irrelevant compositions ? Here comes in, alongside of his almost automatic genius for shapes, the man's superhuman constructive ingenuity. See how he divides that ceiling in such a way that the frames of the separate compositions combine into a huge structure of painted rafters and brackets, nay the Prophets and Sibyls, the Ancestors and Ancestresses themselves, and the naked antique genii, turn into architectural members, holding that imaginary roof together, securing its seeming stability, increasing, by their gesture its upspring and its weightiness, and at the same time determining the tracks along which the eye is forced to travel. Backwards and forwards the eye is driven by that living architecture, round and round in its search now for completion of visible pattern, now for symbolic and narrative meaning. And ever back to the tale of the Creation, so that the remote historic incidents of the Ancestors, the tremendous and tremendously present lyric excitement and despair of the prophetic men and women, the pagan suggestion of the athletic genii, all unite like the simultaneous and consecutive harmonies of a titanic symphony, round the recurrent and dominant phrases of those central stories of how the universe and man were made, so that the beholder has the emotion of hearing not one part of the Old Testament, but the whole of it. But meanwhile, and similarly interchanging and multiplying their imaginative and emotional appeal, the thought of those most memorable of all written stories unites with the perception and empathy of those marvellous systems of living lines and curves and angles, throbbing with their immortal impacts and speeds and directions in a great co-ordinated movement that always begins and never ends, until it seems to the beholder as if those painted shapes were themselves the crowning work of some eighth day of Creation, gathering up in reposeful visible synthesis the whole of Creation's ineffable energy and harmony and splendour.

This example of Michelangelo's ceiling shows how, thanks to the rythmical nature of perception, art fulfils the mission of making us think from Shapes to Things and from Things back to Shapes. And it allows us to see the workings of that psycho-logical law, already manifest in the elementary relations of line to line and dot to dot, by which whatever can be thought and felt in continuous alternation tends to be turned into a whole by such reiteration of common activities. And this means that Art adds to its processes of selection and exclusion a process of *inclusion*, safeguarding æsthetic contemplation by drawing whatever is not wholly refractory into that contemplation's orbit. This turning of non-æsthetic interests from possible competitors and invaders into co-operating allies is an incomparable multiplying factor of æsthetic satisfaction, enlarging the sphere of æsthetic emotion and increasing that emotion's volume and stability by inclusion of just those elements which would have competed to diminish them. The typical instance of such a possible competitor turned into an ally, is that of the cubic element, which I have described (p. 85) as the first and most constant intruder from the thought of *Things* into the contemplation of *Shapes*. For the introduction into a picture of a suggested third dimension is what prevents our *thinking away from* a merely two-dimensional aspect by supplying subsidiary imaginary aspects susceptible of being co-ordinated to it. So perspective and modelling in light and shade satisfy our habit of locomotion by allowing us, as the phrase is, *to go into* a picture ; and *going into*, we remain there and establish on its imaginary planes schemes of horizontals and verticals besides those already existing on the real two-dimensional surface. This addition of shapes due to perspective increases the already existing dramas of empathy, instead of interrupting them by our looking away from the picture, which we should infallibly do if our exploring and so to speak *cubic-locomotor* tendencies were not thus employed inside the picture's limits.

This alliance of æsthetic contemplation with our interest in cubic existence and our constant thought of locomotion, does more however than merely safeguard and multiply our chances of empathic activity. It also increases the sensory discrimination, and hence pleasureableness, of colour, inasmuch as colour becomes, considered as light and shade and *values*, a suggestion of three-dimensional *Things* instead of merely a constituent of two-dimensional *Shapes*. Moreover, one easily tires of " following " verticals and horizontals and their intermediate directions ; while empathic imagination, with its dynamic feelings and frequent semi-mimetic accompaniments, requires sufficient intervals of repose ; and such repose, such alternation of different mental functions, is precisely afforded by thinking in terms of cubic existence. Art-critics have often pointed out what may be called the thinness, the lack of *staying power*, of pictures deficient in the cubic element ; they ought also to have drawn attention to the fatiguing, the almost hallucinatory excitement, resulting from uninterrupted attention to two-dimensional pattern and architectural outlines, which were, indeed, intended to be incidentally looked at in the course of taking stock of the cubic qualities of furniture and buildings.

And since the limits of this volume have restricted me to painting as a type of æsthetic contemplation, I must ask the Reader to accept on my authority and if possible verify for himself, the fact that what I have been saying applies, *mutatis mutandis*, to

the other arts. As we have already noticed, something analogous to a third dimension exists also
in music ; and even, as I have elsewhere shown,[1]
in literature. The harmonies accompanying a
melody satisfy our tendency to think of other notes
and particularly of other allied tonalities ; while
as to literature, the whole handling of words, indeed
the whole of logical thinking, is but a cubic working
backwards and forwards between *what* and *how*,
a co-ordinating of items and themes, keeping the
mind enclosed in one scheme of ideas by forestalling
answers to the questions which would otherwise
divert the attention. And if the realisation of the
third dimension has come to be mistaken for the
chief factor of æsthetic satisfaction, this error is
due not merely to the already noticed coincidence
between cubic imagination and artistic genius,
but even more to the fact that cubic imagination
is the type of the various multiplying factors by
which the empathic, that is to say the essentially
æsthetic, activity, can increase its sphere of operations, its staying power and its intensity.

[1] *The Handling of Words*, English Review, 1911-12.

CHAPTER XVIII

OUR examination has thus proceeded from æsthetic contemplation to the work of Art, which seeks to secure and satisfy it while furthering some of life's various other claims. We must now go back to æsthetic contemplation and find out how the beholder meets these efforts made to secure and satisfy his contemplative attention. For the Reader will by this time have grasped that art can do nothing without the collaboration of the beholder or listener ; and that this collaboration, so far from consisting in the passive " being impressed by beauty " which unscientific æstheticians imagined as analogous to " being impressed by sensuous qualities," by hot or cold or sweet or sour, is in reality a combination of higher activities, second in complexity and intensity only to that of the artist himself.

We have seen in the immediately preceding chapter that the most deliberate, though not the essential, part of the artist's business is to provide against any possible disturbance of the beholder's responsive activity, and of course also to increase by every means that output of responsive activity.

128

But the sources of it are in the beholder, and beyond the control of the most ingenious artistic devices and the most violent artistic appeals. There is indeed no better proof of the active nature of æsthetic appreciation than the fact that such appreciation is so often not forthcoming. Even mere sensations, those impressions of single qualities to which we are most unresistingly passive, are not pleasurable without a favourable reaction of the body's chemistry : the same taste or smell will be attractive or repulsive according as we have recently eaten. And however indomitably colour- and sound-sensations force themselves upon us, our submission to them will not be accompanied by even the most " passive " pleasure if we are bodily or mentally out of sorts. How much more frequent must be lack of receptiveness when, instead of dealing with *sensations* whose intensity depends after all two thirds upon the strength of the outer stimulation, we deal with *perceptions* which include the bodily and mental activities of exploring a shape and establishing among its constituent sensations relationships both to each other and to ourselves ; activities without which there would be for the beholder no shape at all, but mere ragbag chaos !—And in calculating the likelihood of a perceptive empathic response we must remember that such active shape-perception, however instantaneous as compared with

I

the cumbrous processes of locomotion, nevertheless requires a perfectly measurable time, and requires therefore that its constituent processes be held in memory for comparison and coordination, quite as much as the similar processes by which we take stock of the relations of sequence of sounds. All this mental activity, less explicit but not less intense or complex than that of logically "following" an argument, is therefore such that we are by no means always able or willing to furnish it. Not able, because the need for practical decisions hurries us into that rapid inference from a minimum of perception to a minimum of associated experience which we call "recognising things," and thus out of the presence of the perfunctorily dealt with shapes. Not willing, because our nervous condition may be unable for the strain of shape perception ; and our emotional bias (what we call our *interest*) may be favourable to some incompatible kind of activity. Until quite recently (and despite Fechner's famous introductory experiments) æsthetics have been little more than a branch of metaphysical speculation, and it is only nowadays that the bare fact of æsthetic responsiveness is beginning to be studied. So far as I have myself succeeded in doing so, I think I can assure the Reader that if he will note down, day by day, the amount of pleasure he has been able to take in works of art, he will soon recognise the existence of æsthetic responsiveness and its highly variable nature. Should the same Reader develop an interest in such (often humiliating) examination into his own æsthetic experience, he will discover varieties of it which will illustrate some of the chief principles contained in this little book. His diary will report days when æsthetic appreciation has begun with the instant of entering a collection of pictures or statues, indeed sometimes pre-existed as he went through the streets noticing the unwonted charm of familiar objects ; other days when enjoyment has come only after an effort of attention ; others when, to paraphrase Coleridge, *he saw, not felt, how beautiful things are* ; and finally, through other varieties of æsthetic experience, days upon which only shortcomings and absurdities have laid hold of his attention. In the course of such æsthetical self-examination and confession, the Reader might also become acquainted with days whose experience confirmed my never sufficiently repeated distinction between *contemplating Shapes and thinking about Things* ; or, in ordinary æsthetic terminology between *form* and *subject*. For there are days when pictures or statues will indeed afford pleasurable interest, but interest in the things *represented*, not in the *shapes* ; a picture appealing even forcibly to our dramatic or religious or romantic side ; or contrariwise, to our scientific

one. There are days when he may be deeply moved
by a Guido Reni martyrdom, or absorbed in the
" Marriage à la Mode " ; days when even Giorgione's
Pastoral may (as in Rossetti's sonnet) mean nothing
beyond the languid pleasure of sitting on the grass
after a burning day and listening to the plash of
water and the tuning of instruments ; the same
thought and emotion, the same interest and pleasure,
being equally obtainable from an inn-parlour
oleograph. Then, as regards scientific intérest and
pleasure, there may be days when the diarist will
be quite delighted with a hideous picture, because
it affords some chronological clue, or new point of
comparison. " This *dates* such or such a style "—
" *Plein Air* already attempted by a Giottesque !
Degas forestalled by a Cave Dweller ! " etc. etc.
And finally days when the Diarist is haunted by the
thought of what the represented person will do
next : " Would Michelangelo's Jeremiah knock his
head if he got up ? "—" How will the Discobolus
recover when he has let go the quoit ? "—or haunted
by thoughts even more frivolous (though not any
less æsthetically irrelevant !) like " How wonderfully like Mrs So and So ! " " The living image of
Major Blank ! "—" How I detest auburn people with
sealing-wax lips ! " *ad lib*.

Such different *thinkings away from the shapes*
are often traceable to previous orientation of

the thoughts or to special states of body and feelings. But explicable or not in the particular case, these varieties of one's own æsthetic responsiveness will persuade the Reader who has verified their existence, that contemplative satisfaction in shapes and its specific emotion cannot be given by the greatest artist or the finest tradition, unless the beholder meets their efforts more than half way.

The spontaneous collaboration of the beholder is especially indispensable for Æsthetic Empathy. As we have seen, empathic modes of movement and energy and intention are attributed to shapes and to shape elements, in consequence of the modes of movement and energy involved in mere shape perception ; but shape perception does not necessarily call forth empathic imagination. And the larger or smaller dynamic dramas of effort, resistance, reconciliation, cooperation which constitute the most poignant interest of a pictorial or plastic composition, are inhibited by bodily or mental states of a contrary character. We cease to *feel* (although we may continue, like Coleridge, to *see*) that the lines of a mountain or a statue *are rising*, if we ourselves happen to feel as if our feet were of lead and our joints turning to water. The coordinated interplay of empathic movement which makes certain mediæval floor patterns, and also Leonardo's compositions, into whirling harmonies as of a planetary system, cannot take place in our imagination on days of restlessness and lack of concentration. Nay it may happen that arrangements of lines which would flutter and flurry us on days of quiet appreciativeness, will become in every sense "sympathetic" on days when we ourselves feel fluttered and flurried. But lack of responsiveness may be due to other causes. As there are combinations of lines which take longer to perceive because their elements or their coordinating principles are unfamiliar, so, and even more so, are there empathic schemes (or dramas) which baffle dynamic imagination when accustomed to something else and when it therefore meets the new demand with an unsuitable empathic response. Empathy is, even more than mere perception, a question of our activities and therefore of our habits; and the æsthetic sensitiveness of a time and country (say the Florentine fourteenth century) with a habit of round arch and horizontals like that of Pisan architecture, could never take with enthusiasm to the pointed ogeeval ellipse, the oblique directions and unstable equilibrium, the drama of touch and go strain and resistance, of French Gothic; whence a constant readmission of the round arched shapes into the imported style, and a speedy return to the familiar empathic schemes in the architecture of the early Renaissance. On the other hand the persistence of Gothic detail in Northern architecture of the sixteenth and occasionally the seventeenth century, shows how insipid the round arch and straight entablature must have felt to people accustomed to the empathy of Gothic shapes. Nothing is so routinist as imagination and emotion; and empathy, which partakes of both, is therefore more dependent on familiarity than is the perception by which it is started : Spohr, and the other professional contemporaries of Beethoven, probably heard and technically understood all the peculiarities of his last quartets ; but they liked them none the better.

On the other hand continued repetition notoriously begets indifference. We cease to look at a shape which we " know by heart " and we cease to interpret in terms of our own activities and intentions when curiosity and expectation no longer let loose our dynamic imagination. Hence while utter unfamiliarity baffles æsthetic responsiveness, excessive familiarity prevents its starting at all. Indeed both perceptive clearness and empathic intensity reach their climax in the case of shapes which afford the excitement of tracking familiarity in novelty, the stimulation of acute comparison, the emotional ups and downs of expectation and partial recognition, or of recognition when unexpected, the latter having, as we know when we notice that a stranger has the trick of speech or gesture of an acquaintance, a very penetrating emotional warmth. Such discovery of the novel in the familiar, and of the familiar in the new, will be frequent in proportion to the definiteness and complexity of the shapes, and in proportion also to the sensitiveness and steadiness of the beholder's attention ; while on the contrary " obvious " qualities of shape and superficial attention both tend to exhaust interest and demand change. This exhaustion of interest and consequent demand for change unites with the changing non-æsthetic aims imposed on art, together producing innovation. And the more superficial the æsthetic attention given by the beholders, the quicker will style succeed style, and shapes and shape-schemes be done to death by exaggeration or left in the lurch before their maturity ; a state of affairs especially noticeable in our own day.

The above is a series of illustrations of the fact that æsthetic pleasure depends as much on the activities of the beholder as on those of the artist. Unfamiliarity or over-familiarity explain a large part of the æsthetic non-responsiveness summed up in the saying *that there is no disputing of tastes.* And even within the circle of habitual responsiveness to some particular style, or master, there are, as we have just seen, days and hours when an individual beholder's perception and empathic imagination do

not act in such manner as to afford the usual pleasure.
But these occasional, even frequent, lapses must not
diminish our belief either in the power of art or
in the deeply organised and inevitable nature of
æsthetic preference as a whole. What the knowledge of such fluctuations ought to bring home is
that beauty of shape is most spontaneously and
completely appreciated when the attention, instead
of being called upon, as in galleries and concerts,
for the mere purpose of æsthetic enjoyment, is on
the contrary, directed to the artistic or " natural "
beauty of shapes, in consequence of some other
already existing interest. No one except an art-
critic sees a new picture or statue without first
asking " What does it represent ? "; shape-perception
and æsthetic empathy arising incidentally in the
examination which this question leads to. The
truth is that even the art-critic is oftenest brought
into enforced contemplation of the artistic shape by
some other question which arises from his particular bias : By whom ? of what precise date ? "
Even such technical questions as " where and when
restored or repainted ? " will elicit the necessary
output of attention. It is possible and legitimate
to be interested in a work of art for a dozen reasons
besides æsthetic appreciation ; each of these interests
has its own sentimental, scientific, dramatic or
even moneymaking emotion ; and there is no loss

for art, but rather a gain, if we fall back upon one of them when the specific æsthetic response is slow or not forthcoming. Art has other aims besides æsthetic satisfaction ; and æsthetic satisfaction will not come any the quicker for turning our backs upon these non-æsthetic aims. The very worst attitude towards art is that of the holiday-maker who comes into its presence with no ulterior interest or business, and nothing but the hope of an æsthetic emotion which is most often denied him. Indeed such seeking of æsthetic pleasure for its own sake would lead to even more of the blank despondency characteristic of so many gallery goers, were it not for another peculiarity of æsthetic responsiveness, which is responsible for very puzzling effects. This saving grace of the tourist, and (as we shall see) this pitfall of the art-expert, is what I propose to call the *Transferability of Æsthetic Emotion*.

CHAPTER XIX

IN dealing with familiarity as a multiplying factor of æsthetic appreciation, I have laid stress on its effect in facilitating the perception and the empathic interpretation of shapes. But repetition directly affects the emotion which may result from these processes ; and when any emotion has become habitual, it tends to be stored in what we call memory, and to be called forth not merely by the processes in which it originated, but also independently of the whole of them, or in answer to some common or equivalent factor. We are so accustomed to this psychological fact that we do not usually seem to recognise its existence. It is the explanation of the power of words, which, apart from any images they awaken, are often irresistibly evocative of emotion. And among other emotions words can evoke the one due to the easy perception and to the life-corroborating empathic interpretation of shapes. The word *Beautiful*, and its various quasi synonyms, are among the most emotionally suggestive in our vocabulary, carrying perhaps a vague but potent remembrance of our own bodily reaction to the emotion of admiration ; nay even eliciting an incipient rehearsal of the half-parted lips and slightly thrown-back head, the drawn-in breath and wide-opened eyes, with which we are wont to meet opportunities of æsthetic satisfaction. Be this last as it may, it is certain that the emotion connected with the word *Beautiful* can be evoked by that word alone, and without an accompanying act of visual or auditive perception. Indeed beautiful shapes would lose much of their importance in our life, if they did not leave behind them such emotional traces, capable of revival under emotionally appropriate, though outwardly very dissimilar, circumstances ; and thereby enormously increasing some of our safest, perhaps because our most purely subjective, happiness. Instead therefore of despising the raptures which the presence of a Venus of Milo or a Sixtine Madonna can inspire in people manifestly incapable of appreciating a masterpiece, and sometimes barely glancing at it, we critical persons ought to recognise in this funny, but consoling, phenomenon an additional proof of the power of Beauty, whose specific emotion can thus be evoked by a mere name and so transferred from some past experience of æsthetic admiration to a present occasion which would otherwise be mere void and disappointment.

Putting aside these kind of cases, the transfer

(usually accomplished by a word) of the æsthetic emotion, or at least of a willingness for æsthetic emotion, is probably one of the explanations of the spread of æsthetic interest from one art to another, as it is the explanation of some phases of æsthetic development in the individual. The present writer can vouch for the case of at least one real child in whom the possibility of æsthetic emotion, and subsequently of æsthetic appreciation, was extended from music and natural scenery to pictures and statues, by the application of the word *Beautiful* to each of these different categories. And something analogous probably helped on the primæval recognition that the empathic pleasures hitherto attached to geometrical shapes might be got from realistic shapes, say of bisons and reindeer, which had hitherto been admired for their lifelikeness and skill, but not yet subjected to any æsthetic discrimination (*cf.* p. 96). Similarly, in our own times, the delight in natural scenery is being furthered by the development of landscape painting, rather than furthering it. Nay I venture to suggest that it was the habit of the æsthetic emotion such as mediæval men received from the proportions, directions, and coordination of lines in their cathedrals of stone or brick which set their musicians to build up, like Browning's *Abt Vogler*, the soul's first balanced and coordinated dwellings made of sounds.

Be this last as it may, it is desirable that the Reader should accept, and possibly verify for himself, the psychological fact of the *storage and transfer of æsthetic emotion*. Besides, the points already mentioned, it helps to explain several of the cruxes and paradoxes of æsthetics. First and foremost that dictum *De Gustibus non est disputandum* which some philosophers and even æstheticians develop into an explicit denial of all intrinsic shape-preferences, and an assertion that *beautiful* and *ugly* are merely other names for *fashionable* and *unfashionable, original* and *unoriginal,* or *suitable* and *unsuitable.* As I have already pointed out, differences of taste are started by the perceptive and empathic habits, schematically various, of given times and places, and also by those, especially the empathic habits, connected with individual nervous condition : people accustomed to the round arch finding the Gothic one unstable and eccentric ; and, on the other hand, a person taking keen pleasure in the sudden and lurching lines of Lotto finding those of Titian tame and humdrum. But such intrinsically existing preferences and incompatibility are quite enormously increased by an emotional bias for or against a particular kind of art ; by which I mean a bias not due to that art's peculiarities, but preventing our coming in real contact with them.

Æsthetic perception and especially æsthetic

empathy, like other intellectual and emotional activities, are at the mercy of a hostile mental attitude, just as bodily activity is at the mercy of rigidity of the limbs. I do not hesitate to say that we are perpetually refusing to look at certain kinds of art because, for one reason or another, we are emotionally prepossessed against them. On the other hand, once the favourable emotional condition is supplied to us, often by means of words, our perceptive and empathic activities follow with twice the ease they would if the business had begun with them. It is quite probable that a good deal of the enhancement of æsthetic appreciation by fashion or sympathy should be put to the account, not merely of gregarious imitativeness, but of the knowledge that a favourable or unfavourable feeling is " in the air." The emotion precedes the appreciation, and both are genuine.

A more personally humiliating æsthetic experience may be similarly explained. Unless we are very unobservant or very self-deluded, we are all familiar with the sudden checking (often almost physically painful) of our æsthetic emotion by the hostile criticism of a neighbour or the superciliousness of an expert : " Dreadfully old-fashioned," " *Archiconnu*," " second-rate school work," " completely painted over," " utterly hashed in the performance " (of a piece of music), " mere prettiness "—etc.

etc. How often has not a sentence like these turned the tide of honest incipient enjoyment; and transformed us, from enjoyers of some really enjoyable quality (even of such old-as-the hills elements as clearness, symmetry, euphony or pleasant colour!) into shrivelled cavillers at everything save brand-new formulæ and tip-top genius! Indeed, while teaching a few privileged persons to taste the special " quality " which Botticelli has and Botticelli's pupils have not, and thus occasionally intensifying æsthetic enjoyment by distinguishing whatever differentiates the finer artistic products from the commoner, modern art-criticism has probably wasted much honest but shamefaced capacity for appreciating the qualities common, because indispensable, to, all good art. It is therefore not without a certain retributive malignity that I end these examples of the storage and transfer of æsthetic emotion, and of the consequent bias to artistic appreciation, with that of the Nemesis dogging the steps of the connoisseur. We have all heard of some purchase, or all-but-purchase, of a wonderful masterpiece on the authority of some famous expert; and of the masterpiece proving to be a mere school imitation, and occasionally even a certified modern forgery. The foregoing remarks on the storage and transfer of æsthetic emotion, joined with what we have learned about shape-perception and empathy, will enable the Reader to reduce this paradoxical enormity to a natural phenomenon discreditable only when not honestly owned up to. For a school imitation, or a forgery, must possess enough elements in common with a masterpiece, otherwise it could never suggest any connexion with it. Given a favourable emotional attitude and the absence of obvious *extrinsic* (technical or historical) reasons for scepticism, these elements of resemblance must awaken the vague idea, especially the empathic scheme, of the particular master's work, and his name—shall we say Leonardo's ?—will rise to the lips. But *Leonardo* is a name to conjure with, and in this case to destroy the conjurer himself : the word *Leonardo* implies an emotion, distilled from a number of highly prized and purposely repeated experiences, kept to gather strength in respectful isolation, and further heightened by a thrill of initiate veneration whenever it is mentioned. This *Leonardo-emotion*, once set on foot, checks all unworthy doubts, sweeps out of consciousness all thoughts of inferior work (*inferiority* and *Leonardo* being emotionally incompatible !), respectfully holds the candle while the elements common to the imitation and the masterpiece are gone over and over, and the differentiating elements exclusively belonging to Leonardo evoked in the expert's memory, until at last the objective work of art

K

comes to be embedded in recollected masterpieces which impart to it their emotionally communicable virtue. And when the poor expert is finally overwhelmed with ridicule, the Philistine shrewdly decides that a sham Leonardo is just as good as a genuine one, that these are all matters of fashion, and that there is really no disputing of tastes !

CHAPTER XX

ÆSTHETIC IRRADIATION AND PURIFICATION

THE storage and transfer of æsthetic emotion explain yet another fact, with which indeed I began this little book : namely that the word *Beautiful* has been extended from whatever is satisfactory in our contemplation of shapes, to a great number of cases where there can be no question of shapes at all, as in speaking of a " beautiful character " and a " fine moral attitude " ; or else, as in the case of a " beautiful bit of machinery," a " fine scientific demonstration " or a " splendid surgical operation " where the shapes involved are not at all such as to afford contemplative satisfaction. In such cases the word *Beautiful* has been brought over with the emotion of satisfied contemplation. And could we examine microscopically the minds of those who are thus applying it, we might perhaps detect, round the fully-focussed thought of that admirable but nowise *shapely* thing or person or proceeding, the shadowy traces of half-forgotten shapes, visible or audible, forming a halo of real æsthetic experience, and evoked by that word *Beautiful* whose application they partially justify. Nor is this all. Recent psychology teaches that, odd as it at first appears, our more or less definite images, auditive as well as visual, and whether actually perceived or merely remembered, are in reality the intermittent part of the mind's contents, coming and going and weaving themselves on to a constant woof of our own activities and feelings. It is precisely such activities and feelings which are mainly in question when we apply the words *Beautiful* and *Ugly*. Thus everything which has come in connexion with occasions for satisfactory shape-contemplation, will meet with somewhat of the same reception as that shape-contemplation originally elicited. And even the merest items of information which the painter conveys concerning the visible universe ; the merest detail of human character conveyed by the poet ; nay even the mere nervous intoxication furnished by the musician, will all be irradiated by the emotion due to the shapes they have been conveyed in, and will therefore be felt as beautiful.

Moreover, as the " beautiful character " and " splendid operation " have taught us, rare and desirable qualities are apt to be contemplated in a " platonic " way. And even objects of bodily desire, so long as that desire is not acute and pressing, may give rise to merely contemplative longings. All this, added to what has previously been said, sufficiently explains the many and heterogeneous items which are irradiated by the word *Beautiful* and the emotion originally arising from the satisfied contemplation of mere shapes.

And that this contemplation of beautiful shapes should be at once so life-corroborating and so strangely impersonal, and that its special emotion should be so susceptible of radiation and transfer, is sufficient explanation of the elevating and purifying influence which, ever since Plato, philosophers have usually ascribed to the Beautiful. Other moralists however have not failed to point out that art has, occasionally and even frequently, effects of the very opposite kind. The ever-recurrent discussion of this seeming contradiction is, however, made an end of, once we recognise that art has many aims besides its distinguishing one of increasing our contemplation of the beautiful. Indeed some of art's many non-æsthetic aims may themselves be foreign to elevation and purification, or even, as for instance the lewd or brutal subjects of some painting and poetry, and the nervous intoxication of certain music, exert a debasing or enervating influence. But, as the whole of this book has tried to establish, the contemplation of beautiful shapes involves perceptive processes in themselves mentally invigorating and refining, and a play of empathic feelings which realise the greatest desiderata of spiritual life, viz. intensity, purposefulness and

harmony ; and such perceptive and empathic
activities cannot fail to raise the present level of
existence and to leave behind them a higher standard
for future experience. This exclusively elevating
effect of beautiful shape as such, is of course pro-
portioned to the attention it receives and the exclusion of other, and possibly baser, interests connected
with the work of art. On the other hand the
purifying effects of beautiful shapes depend upon
the attention oscillating to and fro between them
and those other interests, e.g. *subject* in the *representative* arts, *fitness* in the *applied* ones, and *expression* in music ; all of which non-æsthetic interests
benefit (enhanced if noble, redeemed if base) by
irradiation of the nobler feelings wherewith they
are thus associated. For we must not forget that
where opposed groups of feeling are elicited, whichever happens to be more active and complex
will neutralise its opponent. Thus, while an even
higher intensity and complexity of æsthetic feelings
is obtained when the " subject " of a picture, the
use of a building or a chattel, or the expression of
a piece of music, is in itself noble ; and a Degas ballet
girl can never have the dignity of a Phidian goddess,
nor a gambling *casino* that of a cathedral, nor the
music to Wilde's Salome that of Brahms' *German
Requiem*, yet whatever of beauty there may be
in the shapes will divert the attention from the

meanness or vileness of the non-æsthetic suggestion. We do not remember the mercenary and libertine allegory embodied in Correggio's *Danae*, or else we reinterpret that sorry piece of mythology in terms of cosmic occurrences, of the Earth's wealth increased by the fecundating sky. Similarly it is a common observation that while *unmusical* Bayreuth-goers often attribute demoralising effects to some of Wagner's music, the genuinely musical listeners are unaware, and usually incredulous, of any such evil possibilities.

This question of the purifying power of the Beautiful has brought us back to our starting-point. It illustrates the distinction between *contemplating an aspect* and *thinking about things*, and this distinction's corollary that shape as such is yon-side of *real* and *unreal*, taking on the character of reality and unreality only inasmuch as it is thought of in connexion with a *thing*. As regards the possibility of being *good* or *evil*, it is evident from all the foregoing that *shape as shape*, and without the suggestion of things, can be evil only in the sense of being ugly, ugliness diminishing its own drawbacks by being, *ipso facto*, difficult to dwell upon, inasmuch as it goes against the grain of our perceptive and empathic activities. The contemplation of beautiful shape is, on the other hand, favoured by its pleasurableness, and such contemplation of beautiful shape lifts our perceptive and empathic activities, that is to say a large part of our intellectual and emotional life, on to a level which can only be spiritually, organically, and in so far, morally beneficial.

CHAPTER XXI

CONCLUSION (EVOLUTIONAL)

SOME of my Readers, not satisfied by the answer implicit in the last chapter and indeed in the whole of this little book, may ask a final question concerning our subject. Not : What is the use of Art ? since, as we have seen, Art has many and various uses both to the individual and to the community, each of which uses is independent of the attainment of Beauty.

The remaining question concerns the usefulness of the very demand for Beauty, of that *Æsthetic Imperative* by which the other uses of art are more or less qualified or dominated. In what way, the Reader may ask, has sensitiveness to Beauty contributed to the survival of mankind, that it should not only have been preserved and established by evolutional selection, but invested with the tremendous power of the pleasure and pain alternative ?

The late William James, as some readers may remember, placed musical pleasure between sentimental love and sea-sickness as phenomena unaccountable by any value for human survival, in fact mysteries, if not paradoxes, of evolution.

The riddle, though not necessarily the mystery, does not consist in the survival of the æsthetic instinct of which the musical one is a mere sub-category, but in the origin and selectional establishment of its elementary constituents, say for instance space-perception and empathy, both of which exist equally outside that instinct which is a mere compound of them and other primary tendencies. For given space-perception and empathy and their capacity of being felt as satisfactory or unsatisfactory, the æsthetic imperative is not only intelligible but inevitable. Instead therefore of asking : Why is there a preference for what we call Beauty ? we should have to ask : why has perception, feeling, logic, imagination, come to be just what it is ? Indeed why are our sense-organs, our bodily structure and chemical composition, what they are ; and why do they exist at all in contradistinction to the ways of being of other living or other inanimate things ? So long as these elementary facts continue shrouded in darkness or taken for granted, the genesis and evolutional reason of the particular compound which we call æsthetic preference must remain only one degree less mysterious than the genesis and evolutional reason of its psychological components.

Meanwhile all we can venture to say is that as satisfaction derived from shapes we call *beautiful*, undoubtedly involves intense, complex, and reiterative mental activities, as it has an undeniable power for happiness and hence for spiritual refreshment, and as it moreover tends to inhibit most of the instincts whose superabundance can jeopardise individual and social existence, the capacity for such æsthetic satisfaction, once arisen, would be fostered in virtue of a mass of evolutional advantages which are as complex and difficult to analyse, but also as deep-seated and undeniable, as itself.

BIBLIOGRAPHY

I. *Lipps.* Raumaesthetik, Leipzig, 1897.

,, Æsthetik, vol. I. part ii., Leipzig, 1906.

II. *Karl Groos.* Æsthetik, Giessen, 1892.

,, ,, Der Æsthetische Genuss, Giessen, 1902.

III. *Wundt.* Physiologische Psychologie (5th Edition, 1903), vol. III. ps. 107 to 209. But the whole volume is full of indirect suggestion on æsthetics.

IV. *Münsterberg.* The Principles of Art Education, New York, 1905. (Statement of Lipps' theory in physiological terms.)

V. *Külpe.* Der gegenwärtige Stand der experimentellen Æsthetik, 1907.

VI. *Vernon Lee and Anstruther-Thomson.* Beauty and Ugliness, 1912 (contains abundant quotations from most of the above works and other sources).

VII. *Ribot.* Le Rôle latent des Images Motrices. Revue Philosophique, March 1912.

VIII. *Witasek.* Psychologie der Raumwahrnehmung des Auges (1910). These two last named are only indirectly connected with visual æsthetics.

For art-evolutional questions consult:

IX. *Haddon.* Evolution in Art, 1895.

X. *Yrjö Hirn.* Origins of Art, Macmillan, 1900.

XI. *Levinstein.* Kinderzeichnungen, Leipzig, 1905.

XII. *Loewy.* Nature in early Greek Art (translation), Duckworth, 1907.

XIII. *Della Seta.* Religione e Arte Figurata, Rome, 1912.

XIV. *Spearing.* The Childhood of Art, 1913.

XV. *Jane Harrison.* Ancient Art and Ritual, 1913.

INDEX